Janice VanCleave's
Science Through the Ages

John Wiley & Sons, Inc.

Dedication

It is my pleasure to dedicate this book to Dr. Tineke Sexton. Dr. Sexton is a teacher of biology and microbiology at Houston Community College Northwest—Houston, Texas. This special person has patiently provided me with answers to my many questions about biology and science in general. This valuable information has made this book even more understandable and fun.

This book is printed on acid-free paper. ∞

Copyright © 2002 by Janice VanCleave. All rights reserved

Illustrations copyright © 2002 by Laurel Aiello. All rights reserved

Published by John Wiley & Sons, Inc., Hoboken, New Jersey
Published simultaneously in Canada

Design and production by Navta Associates, Inc.

The publisher and the author have made every reasonable effort to ensure that the experiments and activities in this book are safe when conducted as instructed but assume no responsibility for any damage caused or sustained while performing the experiments or activities in the book. Parents, guardians, and/or teachers should supervise young readers who undertake the experiments and activities in this book.

Wiley also publishes its books in a variety of electronic formats. Some content that appears in print may not be available in electronic books. For more information about Wiley products, visit our web site at www.wiley.com.

Library of Congress Cataloging-in-Publication Data

VanCleave, Janice Pratt.
   [Science through the ages]
   Janice VanCleave's science through the ages.
      p. cm.
   Includes index.
   Summary: Surveys the development of science and technology through the ages, discussing astronomy, biology, chemistry, earth sciences, physics, and more.
   ISBN 0-471-33097-3 (pbk. : acid-free paper)
     1. Science—History—Juvenile literature. 2. Technology—History—Juvenile literature.
    [1. Science—History. 2. Technology—History.] I. Title: Science through the ages. II. Title.

Q126.4.V36 2001
509—dc21
                                      2001046737

Printed in the United States of America

10 9 8 7 6 5 4 3 2 1

Contents

Acknowledgments

I wish to express my appreciation to these science specialists for their valuable assistance by providing information and/or assisting me in finding it.

Dr. Bonnie J. Buratti, Principal Scientist at the Jet Propulsion Laboratory of the California Institute of Technology. Dr. Buratti conducts research for NASA and serves on the Science teams of NASA Missions to the planets. Dr. Paul Weissman, Senior Research Scientist at the Jet Propulsion Laboratory of the California Institute of Technology. Dr. Weissman does observational and theoretical studies of comets and asteroids, with the objective of trying to understand the origin of the solar system. He also assists with the development of spacecraft missions to comets and asteroids. Larry Wagner, a retired Electrical Systems Designer and amateur achaeologist. A member and past vice-president of the Milwaukee chapter of the Archaeological Institute of America. Mr. Wagner studies have included on site digs as well as "behind the scenes" visits to the Smithsonian and the Field Museum in Chicago.

Members of the Central Texas Astronomical Society, including Johnny Barton, Dick Campbell, John W. McAnally, and Paul Derrick. Johnny is an officer of the club and has been an active amateur astronomer for more than twenty years. Dick is an amateur astronomer who is interested in science education. John is also on the staff of The Association of Lunar and Planetary Observers where he is acting Assistant Coordinator for Transit Timings of the Jupiter Section. Paul is the author of the "Stargazer" column in the *Waco Tribune-Herald.*

Dr. Glenn S. Orton, a Senior Research Scientist at the Jet Propulsion Laboratory of California Institute of Technology. Glenn is an astronomer and space scientist who specializes in investigating the structure and composition of planetary atmospheres. He is best known for his research on Jupiter and Saturn. I have enjoyed exchanging ideas with Glenn about astronomy facts and experiments for modeling astronomy experiments.

Dr. Ben Doughty, head of the department of physics at Texas A & M University—Commerce, in Commerce, Texas. Ben has helped me to better understand the fun of learning about physics. Robert Fanick, a chemist at Southwest Research Institute in San Antonio, Texas, and Virginia Malone, a science assessment consultant.

A special note of gratitude to these educators who assisted by pretesting the activities and/or by providing scientific information: Holly Harris, China Spring Middle School, China Spring, Texas; Anne Skrabanek, home-schooling consultant, Perry, Texas; Connie Chatmas, Sue Dunham, and Stella Cathey, consultants, Marlin, Texas.

Introduction

This book presents fun science facts and projects that relate to the history of science. In the 30 chapters, you'll find discovery experiments and investigations about the different ages of time, and the different science fields, including astronomy, biology, chemistry, earth science, and physics. Some of the chapters look at the invention and development of special scientific instruments, such as telescopes. Others explore the historical development of a scientific topic, such as meteorology. But while the book is divided into sections, the sections and the investigations in them can be performed in any order.

Each chapter explains science terms in simple language that can be easily understood. The information provided is designed to teach facts, concepts, and problem-solving strategies. The scientific concepts are explained in basic terms with little complexity and can be applied to many similar situations. The main objective of the book is to present the fun of science. You are encouraged to learn through exploration and literature connections.

HOW TO USE THIS BOOK

You can start at the beginning of any section of the book, or you can just flip through the chapters for a topic that sounds interesting. Before you do any of the chapter investigations, read them through completely. Once you've decided on an investigation to try, collect all the needed materials and follow all procedures carefully. The format for each chapter is as follows:

- **Did You Know?** A fun fact that identifies the focus of the chapter. This statement is followed by an explanation of the science behind the fact.

- **Fun Time!** A discovery experiment related to the fun fact. Each experiment includes a complete list of easy-to-find **Materials,** a step-by-step **Procedure,** a section identifying the expected **Results,** and a **Why?** section that explains why the experiment works.

- **More Fun with . . . !** An additional fun activity relating to the topic.

- **Book List** A list of other books about the topic, both fiction and nonfiction.

GENERAL INSTRUCTIONS FOR THE EXPERIMENTS

1. Read each experiment completely before starting.

2. Collect supplies. You will have less frustration and more fun if all the materials necessary for the experiment are ready before you start. You lose your train of thought when you have to stop and search for supplies. Ask an adult for advice before substituting any materials.

3. Do not rush. Follow each step very carefully; never skip steps, and do not add your own. Safety is of the utmost importance, and by reading each experiment before starting, then following the instructions exactly, you can feel confident that no unexpected results will occur.

4. Observe. If your results are not the same as those described in the experiment, carefully reread the instructions and start over from step 1.

I

PAST TO PRESENT

History of Science

DID YOU KNOW?

You could lift a horse with your finger!

Science is a system of knowledge about the nature of the things in the **universe** (Earth and all natural objects in space regarded as a whole). **Astronomy** is the study of **celestial bodies** (natural things in the sky, such as stars, suns, moons, and planets). **Biology** is the study of **organisms** (living things, such as plants and animals). **Chemistry** is the study of the materials that substances are made of and how they change and combine. **Earth science** is the study of the Earth. **Physics** is the study of energy and matter and how they interact. **Energy** is the ability to cause motion, and matter is anything that can be moved. **Matter** takes up space and has **mass** (an amount of material).

People began thinking about and doing science thousands of years ago, before they even developed a system of writing. So there is no written record of the first investigations. But some of the earliest drawings indicate observations of the natural world, such as the rising and setting of the Sun, phases of the Moon, and fire. (See chapter 7 for more on phases.) Like many of today's scientific discoveries, the "discovery" of fire was serendipitous, which means it was accidental. The first observed fire was most likely created by lightning. One can only guess at the observations made at the time, but getting burned was probably one of them. Fire was one of humans' most important early discoveries. It changed the way people lived and the way societies developed. With fire, not only could people stay warm, but they could also cook and keep their food longer.

The ancient people who made the greatest contributions to Western science were the Greeks. Greek **philosophers** (people who study the meaning of life, problems of right and wrong, and how we know things) made many observations of the natural world and developed theories (ideas) to explain things they saw. Pythagoras of Samos (c.580–c.500 B.C.), a Greek philosopher and religious leader, was responsible for important developments in the history of mathematics and astronomy. Aristotle (384–322 B.C.) was the most influential philosopher in the history of Western thought. Centuries after his death, the writings of Aristotle were considered the truth by the Christian church, and to disagree with his ideas was a crime punishable by imprisonment or death. The study of the natural sciences was dominated by Aristotle until early modern times. While Aristotle and most other Greek scholars were thinkers, some, such as the Greek mathematician Archimedes (c.298–212 B.C.), also performed experiments.

In the past as well as now, scientific advancements occurred out of the need to solve problems. One common problem was the movement of heavy objects, such as large rocks. A **machine** is a tool used to make it easier to move things. One of the first simple machines used to move a load was the lever. A **lever** is any rigid bar, such as a tree limb, that turns about a support called a **fulcrum.** The lever was used for thousands of years before Archimedes explained how it worked. From his investigations, Archimedes determined that if you had a long enough lever you could lift anything, even a horse by pushing down on one end of the lever with one finger. (The problem, of course, is getting a lever strong enough and long enough, but in theory it is true, as you'll see in the investigation that follows.)

From the fall of Rome in A.D. 476 until about the mid-1500s, there was little advancement in science. Most contributions to science during this period were made by people interested in **alchemy** (a mixture of science and magic that dealt with changing less valuable metals into gold and finding ways to prolong life indefinitely). **Alchemists** were people who practiced alchemy. The results of the investigations of many alchemists became the foundations for chemistry and **pharmacology** (the study of medicines).

The rebirth of science occurred around 1543 with the publication of two books. The first book was written by the Polish astronomer Nicolaus Copernicus (1473–1543). Before his book, many scientists thought the Earth was the center of the universe. Copernicus suggested that it was not. (See chapter 6 for more on Copernicus and models of the universe.) The second book was about human **anatomy** (the study of the structure of organisms). This book was written by the Belgian **anatomist** (scientist who studies anatomy) Andreas Vesalius (1514–1564). Before Vesalius, human anatomy was based on thoughts rather than observations. Vesalius dissected human **cadavers** (dead bodies) and his careful descriptions of human anatomy helped establish modern observational science. (See chapter 12 for more on Vesalius and anatomy.)

In the late sixteenth century, the English philosopher Francis Bacon (1561–1626) made a lasting contribution to science. He described what he called the inductive method, now commonly called the **scientific method** (the process of thinking through possible solutions to a problem and testing each possibility to find the best solution). The scientific method involves the following: doing **research** (a process of collecting information about a topic being studied), identifying the **problem** (a scientific question to be solved), coming up with a **hypothesis** (an idea about the solution to the problem), designing and conducting an **experiment** (a procedure to test the hypothesis), collecting and organizing **data** (observations and/or measured facts), and reaching a **conclusion** (a statement relating the results to the hypothesis).

Today, scientists have sent people to the Moon and, with various instruments, can look inside a living human body. But in spite of all the advancements of science, there are still many unsolved problems. There is so much more to be learned about the universe and organisms in it. Maybe you will make your own great discoveries.

FUN TIME!

Purpose

To demonstrate a lever.

Materials

egg-size piece of modeling clay
ruler
index card

Procedure

1. Break the clay into four pieces as close to the same size as possible.

2. Mold the clay into four balls.

3. Lay the ruler on a table. Place one clay ball at one end of the ruler and two clay balls, one in front of the other, at the opposite end.

4. Lay the index card on the table and the fourth clay ball in the center of the card. The clay is a support.

5. Position the ruler on the clay support so that it balances. Make note of the length of the ruler on both sides of the clay support. *NOTE: If you have difficulty balancing the ruler, slightly flatten the top of the clay support.*

Results

From the point where the ruler balances, it is longer to the end with one clay ball than to the end with two clay balls.

Why?

The place where the ruler is supported by the clay represents a fulcrum, the point about which a lever (the ruler) turns. If equal weights were placed on opposite ends of a lever, the lever would balance with the fulcrum in the center. But if unequal weights were place on the ends of the lever, as in this investigation, the fulcrum would have to be closer to the heavier weight to balance the lever.

The distance a weight is from the fulcrum is called the **lever arm.** When the fulcrum is not in the center of the lever, but is placed closer to one end, the result is two unequal lever arms, one short and the other long. It takes less weight on the long lever arm to bal-

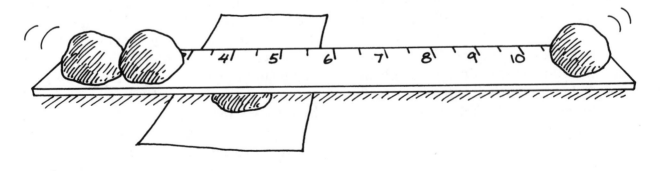

ance a heavier weight on the short lever arm. Archimedes said that if he had a place to stand and a long enough lever, he could lift the Earth.

MORE FUN WITH BALANCE!

Make a balancing bee by copying or tracing the bee pattern on this page. Glue the pattern to stiff paper, such as poster board. When the glue has dried, cut out the bee.

Make two separate chains with three paper clips in each chain. Attach one chain to the end of each wing. Take a new pencil with a flat eraser and hold it vertically in one hand (eraser end up). Hold the bee horizontally in the other hand. Place the tip of the bee's nose in the center of the eraser and release the bee. The bee stands on its nose. If it leans to one side, adjust the position of the paper clip chains. This will change the length of the lever arms, the distance the chains are from the fulcrum (the bee's nose). As with the ruler in the original investigation, the length of the lever arms affects how the bee balances.

BOOK LIST

Hann, Judith. *How Science Works*. Pleasantville, N.Y.: The Reader's Digest Association, 1991. Interesting facts and activities about levers and other science topics.

Richards, Roy. *101 Science Tricks*. New York: Sterling, 1990. Fun experiments about levers and other science topics with everyday materials.

VanCleave, Janice. *Janice VanCleave's Machines*. New York: Wiley, 1993. Experiments about levers and other machines. Each chapter contains ideas that can be turned into award-winning science fair projects.

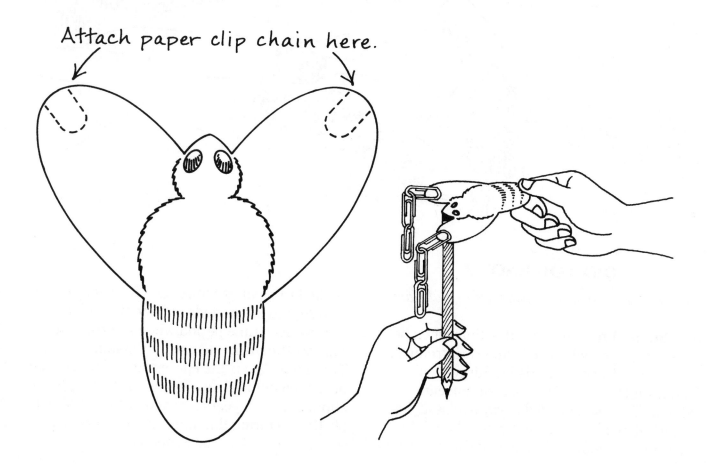

Attach paper clip chain here.

2

Stone Age

DID YOU KNOW?

You can use Stone Age–style tools to make art!

The **Stone Age** was a period of time when people used stone tools. The term was introduced in the early 1800s by Christian Jürgensen Thomsen (1788–1865), a Danish museum curator. Thomsen needed a way of classifying historical materials, so he divided them into three groups: stone, bronze, and iron. He later applied the names Stone Age, Bronze Age, and Iron Age to the periods of history. Each age represents a time period when a certain material was the main one used for making tools. The Stone Age is the earliest and longest stage of human cultural development, starting from about 2 million years ago and lasting to about 5000 B.C. During that time, stones were used for tools as well as for weapons.

Around 5000 B.C., the peoples of Mesopotamia (an area that corresponds to modern Iraq) and Egypt started using metal tools, but there were many regions of the world that still used stone tools when Columbus discovered America in 1492. While most of the world today works with metal and high-tech tools—everything from hammers to computers—there are still a few cultures, such as some Aborigines in Australia, who use stone tools just as their ancient ancestors did in the Stone Age.

FUN TIME!

Purpose

To use Stone Age–style tools to make a drawing.

Materials

round wooden toothpick

2 rocks—1 large and flat, 1 small and lemon-size (A nonporous cutting board can be used instead of the large rock)

1 tablespoon (15 mL) dirt

spoon

3-ounce (90-mL) paper cup

tap water

sheet of white construction paper

Procedure

1. Use the following steps to make a stick paintbrush:

   • Lay the toothpick on the large flat rock.

   • Using the smaller rock, beat one end of the toothpick until it is frayed like bristles of a paintbrush.

   CAUTION: Hold the rock in one hand and keep the other hand away so you do not hit your fingers.

2. Use the following steps to make dirt paint:

   • Place the dirt in the center of the large flat rock.

   • Use the smaller rock to grind the dirt into a fine powder.

   • Use the spoon to scoop the ground dirt into the paper cup.

   • Add a little water to the ground dirt in the cup and stir to make a thick paint.

3. Using the stick paintbrush and dirt paint, make simple drawings on the paper that tell a story or convey a message.

Results

You used stones as tools to make a paintbrush and paint, and then you made a story picture.

Why?

The first humans used natural **pigments** (coloring matter), such as different colored dirt, to make paint. This paint was used to decorate their bodies and their homes as well as to tell stories, as in the story pictures drawn on the walls of cave dwellings. The oldest known cave drawings, discovered in Namibia, Africa, are believed to have been drawn about 24,000 B.C. These drawings on the rocky cave walls are called **petroglyphs** (carvings or line drawings on rock).

People still decorate their bodies and homes with paint. But few make stick brushes and mud paint using stone tools. Instead, many pigments are chemically produced. These colors are mixed with water, oil, and/or waxes to form body paints such as lipsticks, and decorative art paints such as acrylics.

MORE FUN WITH STONE TOOLS!

Plant parts, such as leaves and flowers, contain pigments. Leaves generally have green pigment and flowers have different colored pigments. If the plant parts are crushed, their pigments can be used to stain cloth. Use a rock to crush plant parts and decorate a T-shirt.

- Fold two to four sheets of newspaper and place them inside a white T-shirt.

- Lay the shirt on a nonporous cutting board so that the front of the shirt is faceup.

- Arrange flower petals and leaves on the shirt front. Make small piles of petals and leaves to create a design.

- Cover the flower parts with waxed paper, and crush the parts by tapping them with a rock. Use caution as before when using the stone tool.

- Remove the waxed paper and crushed flower parts. Allow the shirt to dry. *NOTE: Washing the shirt by hand in cold water will help keep the colors bright.*

BOOK LIST

Arnold, Caroline. *Stone Age Farmers beside the Sea: Scotland's Prehistoric Village of Skara Brae.* New York: Clarion Books, 1997. Describes life in the prehistoric Scottish Village of Skara Brae, where the community farmed, herded, hunted, and fished from 3100 to 2500 B.C.

MacDonald, Fiona. *The Stone Age News.* Cambridge, Mass.: Candlewick Press, 1998. Uses a newspaper format to present fictional articles, interviews, eyewitness accounts, and even advertisements that feature the history of the Stone Age.

VanCleave, Janice. *Help! My Science Project is Due Tomorrow!* Hoboken, N.J.: Wiley, 2002. Easy science projects, including those about pigments.

Bronze Age

DID YOU KNOW?

An accidental mixing of metals changed history!

Metallurgy is the science of metals, including understanding the properties of different metals, removing metals from rocks, and working with metals. Metallurgy began in Mesopotamia around 3000 B.C. The earliest metals used were probably native gold and copper. **Native metals** naturally occur in pure form, meaning they are not combined with other substances. Gold was extracted from streambeds, and copper that had been washed out of gravel was found on or near the surface.

At first the use of metals was limited to what could be made by a Stone Age technique now called **cold forging. Forging** is generally the method of shaping a heated metal by hammer-ing. The original cold forging involved hammer-ing cold metals into shapes with a stone. Later two different steps of working with metals led to the production of alloys. An **alloy** is a mixture of two or more metals or of one or more metals and a nonmetal, particularly carbon. These steps are called annealing and smelting. **Annealing** makes metals more **malleable** (capable of being shaped by hammering) as the result of a slow, softening heat. **Smelting** involves more heat, which melts metals. The molten (melted) metals can be **cast,** or poured into molds for desired shapes, after cooling.

At some point, early metalworkers might have accidentally or purposely poured two molten metals in a mold, causing them to mix and form an alloy. Because alloys have better properties than native metals alone, this act of mixing molten metals led to experimenting with different combinations. Early alloy forms used in abundance were made of copper combined with arsenic and antimony. Eventually people discovered that mixing copper and tin produced **bronze,** a stronger, more easily shaped alloy that is still used today.

Bronze changed history in many ways. One change was that bronze was used to make many, better tools than stone. Another change was that the scarcity of tin in Mesopotamia led to explorations into new lands in search of it. Other changes involved improvements in mining, smelting, and casting. Because bronze was such an important discovery, the time when people used bronze tools is called the **Bronze Age.**

As with other periods in history, the Bronze Age occurred at different times in different parts of the world, and not at all in some. For example, archaeological discoveries in Thailand indicate that bronze technology was known there as early as 4500 B.C., while some parts of Africa basically bypassed the Bronze Age, going straight from the Stone Age to the Iron Age. (See chapter 4 for more on the Iron Age.)

FUN TIME!

Purpose

To compare the properties of native copper with a copper alloy.

Materials

wire cutters
4-inch (10-cm) or longer piece of 16- or 18-gauge copper wire (available at hardware stores)
new penny

Procedure

1. Use the wire cutters to remove any insulation from the wire.

2. With your hands, test the malleability of the copper wire. Do this by trying to bend the wire back and forth once.

3. Now try bending the penny back and forth.

Results

The penny doesn't bend, but the wire does.

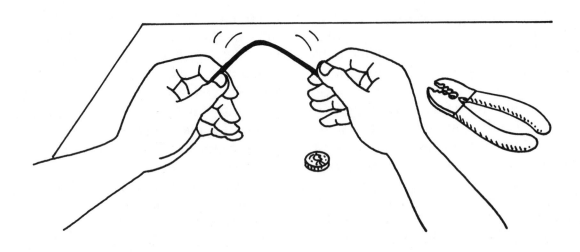

Why?

The wire is made of copper while the coin is an alloy of copper. The shape of the wire and the penny is not the same, so exact comparisons of the malleability of the wire and the coin cannot be made. But since the thickness of the wire and the coin is similar, it can be determined that native copper is more malleable than a copper alloy.

MORE FUN WITH COPPER WIRE!

Copper wire, with and without colored insulation, can be used to make a wire sculpture. Insulated telephone cable contains separate wires covered with different colors of insulation. Use these wires or others (available at hardware stores) and plaster of paris to make your sculpture. First, shape the wires into the desired shape. Then, in a paper cup, mix the plaster and water as directed on the container. Stir the plaster with a craft stick. When the plaster starts to get hard, stick the ends of the wires into the plaster to make a stand for your sculpture. Allow the plaster to harden, then peel off the paper cup. *CAUTION: Do not wash plaster down the drain because it can clog the drain.*

BOOK LIST

Chisholm, Jane. *Timelines of World History.* New York: Scholastic, 2000. Outlines historical events of different time periods, including the Bronze Age.

Soucie, Gary. *What's the Difference between Lenses and Prisms and Other Scientific Things?* New York: Wiley, 1995. Provides interesting information about materials made of copper, brass, and bronze.

4

Iron Age

DID YOU KNOW?

Prehistoric people used iron from outer space!

Native iron may have been known since **prehistory** (the time before written records appeared, which occurred about 3000 B.C.). This iron most likely came to Earth from **meteorites** (rocks form space that hit Earth's surface), because most iron on Earth is combined with other substances in rocks. Ancient writings refer to the "metal of heaven," which is believed to have been iron in meteorites striking Earth. In addition to finding iron in meteorites, a serendipitous discovery of iron

may have occurred when fires were built on land containing iron ore. (An **ore** is a rock that contains enough metal to make it profitable to **extract,** or remove, the metal.) When exceptionally hot fires were produced, some of the iron in the ore melted and combined with sand in the earth, producing a type of iron alloy now called **wrought iron.** The sand formed glasslike threads throughout the iron, making even cooled wrought iron more malleable and more resistant to rusting than native iron or other kinds of iron alloys.

Crude **steel** (an iron alloy made of iron and carbon) was produced at least 2,000 years ago. To make this steel, scraps of iron and **char-**

coal (a carbon material) were placed in a pot made of fire-resistant clay which was heated. This process is the oldest method of making steel. But it was so difficult to melt the iron that only small amounts of steel could be made. The heat of the fire was usually not hot enough to melt the iron; it only made the iron soft enough to forge (to shape by heating and hammering). Forging not only shaped the metal but changed its grain size, making the metal stronger and more **ductile** (able to be drawn into a wire).

At first, fires to heat iron ore were made hotter by blowing air on them through hollow tubes. Later, **bellows** (a device used for producing a strong gust of air) was used to force air into the fire. Around 1500 B.C., Egyptians used bellows made of goat skin to force air into fires and make them hot. But even with these techniques, the fires were usually only hot enough to soften but not melt the iron. A simple air blast furnace was made by the Spanish in the 700s. The **blast furnace** gets its name from the steady blast of air that is forced into the lower part of the furnace. This crude blast furnace melted small amounts of iron, that could be used to produce wrought iron.

Around 1400, a blast furnace was made that could melt large amounts of iron, but wrought iron was so inexpensive that it remained the main form of iron used. Not until the late 1800s was high-quality, inexpensive steel made. This was made possible by the Bessemer furnace, a blast furnace named after its British inventor, Henry Bessemer (1813–1898).

The ability to remove iron from iron ore marked the beginning of the **Iron Age** (period when iron tools were used). The Iron Age began about 1100 B.C. in Asia Minor (the Asian part of Turkey). The Iron Age, like the Stone Age and the Bronze Age, did not happen everywhere at once. Instead the knowledge of how to extract iron and make it into tools spread from one place to another. The Iron Age

appeared in China by about 600 B.C. In Africa, iron objects found in tombs date from the sixth century B.C. Ironworking was unknown in the New World until the arrival of the Europeans in the sixteenth century.

The best thing about iron was its cheapness. Because iron ore is abundant and widespread, suddenly everyone could afford metal tools. Today, iron and steel are used to make thousands of products important in our lives, ranging from paper clips to spacecraft.

FUN TIME!

Purpose

To identify products made with iron or an iron alloy.

Materials

magnet
pencil and paper

Procedure

1. Touch the magnet to as many different items around your home as possible. What sticks to the magnet? *CAUTION: Do not touch audio- and videotapes, computer disks, credit cards, TV and computer screens. Magnets can damage these items.* (See chapters 24 and 28 for more information about magnets.)

2. Record your results in a table like the one shown here. Make a note in the table if only part of an item sticks to the magnet, such as the metal band around a pencil eraser.

Results

Some metal items stick to the magnet, but nonmetals do not.

Response to a Magnet		
Item	Sticks	Doesn't Stick
Refrigerator	yes	
Pencil	metal on pencil only	wood, eraser, and pencil lead

using pieces of pipe cleaners and straws. Do this by cutting 12-inch (30-cm) pipe cleaners into three 4-inch (10-cm) pieces. Cut the straws into desired lengths. To connect two straw pieces, bend the pipe cleaner piece. Insert ends into one end of each straw piece. Adjust the angle between the straw pieces as desired by bending the pipe cleaner connector, as shown.

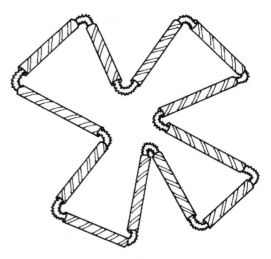

WHY?

A **magnet** is an object that can attract **magnetic materials** (materials attracted to or turned into a magnet, such as iron and steel). Iron is magnetic, and many metal items around the home are made of steel, which is an alloy of iron. So your magnet sticks to objects made of iron or steel.

MORE FUN WITH IRON!

Pipe cleaners have two thin steel wires running through them. These wires are twisted around short pieces of fiber that make the pipe cleaner fuzzy. The wire is thin enough to be flexible. Make models of flowers or animals

BOOK LIST

Fitzgerald, Karen. *The Story of Iron.* New York: Franklin Watts, 1997. Tells how important iron has been throughout history and the role it plays in our lives today.

VanCleave, Janice. *Help! My Science Project is Due Tomorrow!* Hoboken, N.J.: Wiley 2002. Easy science projects, including those about meteorites.

VanCleave, Janice. *Janice VanCleave's Magnets.* New York: Wiley, 1993. Experiments about magnets. Each chapter contains ideas that can be turned into award-winning science fair projects.

Industrial Age

DID YOU KNOW?

Young children once ran machines in factories!

The **Industrial Age** was a time of incredible development in **technology** (the use of scientific knowledge to make useful items). This period began in the late 1700s in Great Britain, and by the mid-1800s it was widespread in Europe and the northeastern United States. It was called industrial because it had to do with manufacturing, which means the making of every kind of useful material, from thread to great machines. This time is often called the Industrial Revolution because the changes to every aspect of people's lives were so great.

The principal sudden change made during this age was the introduction of more powerful machines. Before this time, manufacturing was done by hand or simple machines powered by sources such as windmills or waterwheels. These power sources do not create the power; instead they are **turbines,** or wheels that change the force of moving **fluids** (gases and liquids), such as wind and water, into **mechanical energy** (energy of motion). Basically the moving water or wind hits the blades on the turbines, causing the blades and the shaft on which they are attached to **rotate** (turn around a center point). This motion or mechanical energy is used to turn other parts of a machine. The machines invented during the Industrial Revolution needed more power than the simple waterwheels or windmills of the day could provide. One of the first sources of power was steam. Later chemical energy, such as oil, gasoline, and electrical energy, was used as power. Today, improved water turbines are used to generate electricity, and steam turbines are among the most powerful machines in the world.

The Industrial Revolution took manufacturing out of the home and small workshops. The new, more powerful machines replaced handwork. They do so much of the work that unskilled workers could be used to run them. Even young children from poor families were sent to operate the machines in large factories. The working conditions were often hard and dangerous. Later, after word spread of the terrible conditions, child labor laws were passed that prevented the hiring of young children. The positive part of the revolution was the great increase in the production of goods that improved the way people lived.

FUN TIME!

Purpose

To demonstrate how to increase the effectiveness of a turbine.

Materials

scissors
ruler
sheet of paper
pencil
large coin (quarter)

one-hole paper punch
modeling clay
drinking straw

Procedure

1. Cut a 6-by-6-inch (15-by-15-cm) square from the sheet of paper.

2. Draw two diagonal lines across the paper square so that you have an X.

3. Use the coin to draw a circle in the center of the square.

4. Punch one hole in each corner of the square as shown.

5. Poke a hole through the center of the circle with the point of the pencil.

6. Use the scissors to cut along the four diagonal lines, from the corners to the edge of the center circle. These sections will be the blades of your pinwheels.

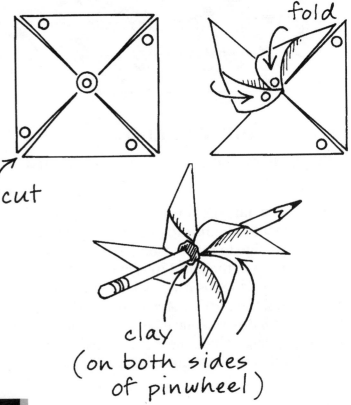

7. Make a paper wheel. To do this, fold the blades toward the center, one at a time clockwise, aligning all the corner holes with the hole in the center of the paper.

8. Push the pencil through the holes, and position the paper wheel in the center of the pencil. Add pieces of modeling clay to both sides of the paper to hold the wheel in place. You have made a pinwheel.

9. Cradle the ends of the pencil in the hollow between the index finger and thumb of each hand, palms facing, as shown. Do not grip the pencil.

10. Ask your helper to stand about 12 inches (30 cm) from the pinwheel and to blow as hard as possible toward the blades. Observe the speed at which the pinwheel turns. Repeat at about 6 inches (15 cm).

11. Repeat step 10 with your helper blowing through the straw toward the blades.

Results

The wheel and pencil turn together when air is blown on the blades. The pinwheel turns faster when air is blown through the straw.

Why?

The force of the air striking the paper blades makes the wheel turn. Since the wheel fits tightly on the pencil, the pencil turns as the wheel turns. A turbine used to provide power is made up of a series of blades on a shaft. Like the turning pencil, the shaft of a turbine turns as the wheel turns. This turning shaft is used to turn other parts of a machine.

Only part of the air blown toward your pinwheel actually hit the paper blades. Using the straw directed more of the air toward the blades and thus caused them to turn faster. Modern turbines are in a closed container so that the entering fluid has to hit the blades of

the turbine. This design increased the amount of energy available to turn the blades, thus increasing the effectiveness of the turbine.

MORE FUN WITH TURBINES!

Your pinwheel can be used to lift an object. Attach one end of a 2-foot (60-cm) piece of sewing thread about 2 inches (5 cm) from one end of the pencil. Tie the free end of the thread to a paper clip. Hold the pinwheel as before and blow toward the blades. Observe the movement of the paper clip.

BOOK LIST

Kelly, John. *Everyday Machines*. Atlanta: Turner Publishing, 1995. The ins and outs of common machines.

Parker, Steve. *How Things Work*. New York: Random House, 1991. Explains of many power-driven machines, as well as the fundamentals of turbine power.

VanCleave, Janice. *Janice VanCleave's Machines*. New York: Wiley, 1993. Experiments about machines, including turbines. Each chapter contains ideas that can be turned into award-winning science fair projects.

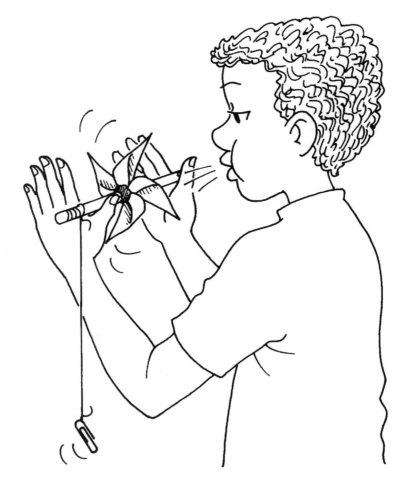

II

ASTRONOMY

6

The Universe

DID YOU KNOW?

Some ancient people thought Earth rested on the back of a giant turtle!

Astronomy is the study of celestial bodies, which are natural things in the sky, such as stars, suns, moons, and planets. Observations of the sky probably date from prehistoric times, so astronomy is one of the oldest sciences. One ancient idea about the universe was that Earth rested on the back of a giant turtle. The motion of the turtle seemed to explain why Earth shook at times during what we now know to be earthquakes.

Cosmology is the branch of astronomy that deals with the study of the universe as a whole, including distant past and its future. Some

ancient astronomers viewed the universe as being relatively small and basically made up of a flat Earth surrounded by a domelike shell with the Sun, Moon, and stars on it. As time passed, people's views of the size of the universe increased. Today it is considered **infinite** (without limits).

Early views of the universe put Earth at the center. This is called a **geocentric** (Earth-centered) model. The Greek philosopher Aristotle (384–322 B.C.) supported the geocentric view, and his ideas about the universe were considered true by most people for almost 2,000 years. Another influential, Roman astronomer was Ptolemy (A.D. 100–170). Little is known of Ptolemy's life, but he made astronomical observations from Alexandria, Egypt, during the years 127–141 and probably spent most of his life there. Ptolemy agreed with Aristotle's geocentric view of the universe, and proposed a model of a motionless Earth with the known celestial bodies **orbiting** (moving in a curved path about another body) in the order of Moon, Mercury, Venus, Sun, Mars, Jupiter, and Saturn.

No one seriously questioned Ptolemy's theory until 1543, when the Polish astronomer Nicolaus Copernicus (1473–1543) published a book suggesting that the Sun was the center of the universe. This is called a **heliocentric** (Sun-centered) model. Copernicus was not the first to view the universe as Sun-centered. The Greek astronomer Aristarchus of Samos (fl. c.270 B.C.) had introduced the idea almost 2,000 years previously, but few accepted it. The mathematician Thomas Digges (d.1595) was one of the earliest English supporters of the Copernican theory. He not only supported a Sun-centered universe but also introduced the idea of an infinite universe with stars spread throughout. (**Stars** are large celestial bodies made of very hot, glowing gases.)

The first decisive step toward a modern model of the universe was made early in the seventeenth century, when the Italian astronomer Galileo Galilei (1564–1642) used his homemade telescopes to closely observe the stars and planets, in particular the moons of Jupiter orbiting that planet. What he observed supported Copernicus's heliocentric model of the universe. Because the church held that Earth was the center of creation, Galileo was condemned as a **heretic** (someone who publicly disagrees with beliefs of the church) in 1633 and imprisoned in his own house.

Other supporters of the Copernican model of the universe were the German astronomer Johannes Kepler (1571–1630), who described the shape of the **orbit** (the curved path of one body moving around another) of each planet using the data collected by Danish astronomer

Tycho Brahe (1546–1601), and English physicist Sir Isaac Newton (1642–1727), who explained that **gravity** (the force of attraction between all objects in the universe) keeps planets in orbit. By the end of the 1600s, the heliocentric model was generally accepted by astronomers. Today it is known that our **solar system** (a group of celestial bodies that orbit a star called a sun) is a very tiny part of a **galaxy** (a group made up of millions of stars, gas, and dust) called the Milky Way, and that this galaxy is just one of many galaxies in the universe. Our Sun is not the center of the universe.

FUN TIME!

Purpose

To make a model that shows Ptolemy's view of the universe.

Materials

yardstick (meterstick)
22-by-28-inch (55-by-70-cm) piece of poster board
pencil
26-inch (65-cm) piece of string
marker

Procedure

1. Lay the yardstick (meterstick) across the middle of the poster board, parallel with the long sides.

2. Using the pencil and the measuring stick, make nine small dots on the poster board 3 inches (7.5 cm) apart. The first dot will be 3 inches (25 cm) from the left edge of the poster board; the last dot will be 1 inch (2.5 cm) from the edge of the poster board.

3. Tie a loop in one end of the string.

4. Place the pencil point through the loop and position the point on the second dot from the left side of the paper. With your other hand, pull the string outward over the first dot. Hold the string on the first dot with your thumb as you move the pencil like a compass across the poster board to draw a circle.

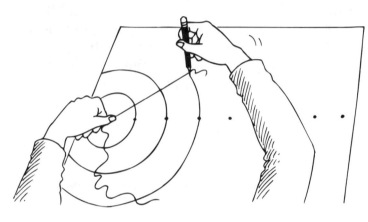

5. Repeat step 4 for each of the remaining dots, drawing as much of a circle as will fit on the board for each dot.

6. Using the marker, draw circles at each dot and add labels to represent the planets as shown. Draw stars in the rightmost band to represent the space beyond Saturn.

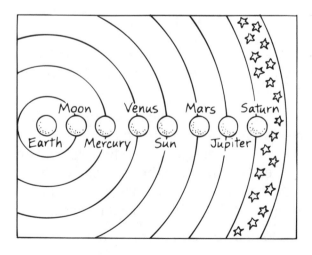

Results

You have made a geocentric model that shows how Ptolemy thought the universe was organized.

Why?

Ptolemy believed that in relation to their starry background, the Sun and the Moon moved in a straight line in their paths across the sky, while other celestial bodies seemed to wander. Thus, these wandering celestial bodies were called **planets** (celestial bodies that orbit a sun) from the Greek word for "wanderers." Today's model of the universe is not geocentric. But the solar system is heliocentric, with nine planets orbiting the Sun.

MORE FUN WITH THE UNIVERSE!

The Milky Way Galaxy is a giant spiral of several billion stars, one of which is our Sun. Its true shape, size, and nature were discovered by astronomers only in the twentieth century. If it were possible to view our galaxy from above, it would look like a spinning pinwheel; from the side it would look flat and disklike, much like a CD with a swollen center. Our solar system lies within one of the spiral arms and is speeding around the center of the galaxy at about 563,000 miles (900,800 km) per hour. It takes about 200 million years for the solar system to make one complete revolution.

All the stars you see from Earth are part of the Milky Way Galaxy. When you look toward either edge of the galaxy as shown by the arrows in the figure, you are looking through the greatest number of stars. Most of these stars appear as a faint, irregular ribbon of light that spans the sky. This is ribbon called the Milky Way because early observers thought it looked like spilled milk.

THE MILKY WAY GALAXY

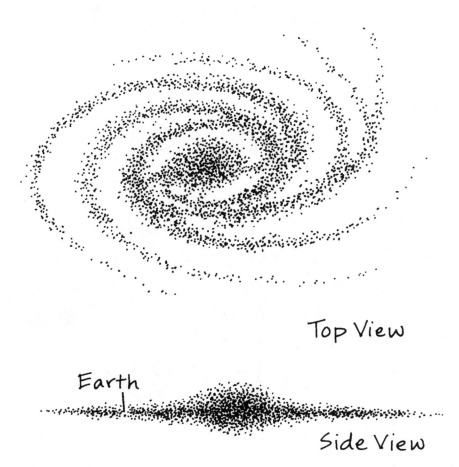

Top View

Earth

Side View

The Milky Way is visible on most nights that are clear and moonless. If you look for the Milky Way on different nights during the year, you will discover that it changes position in the sky. This shows how Earth moves and our view of the galaxy changes.

BOOK LIST

Filkin, David. *Stephen Hawking's Universe*. New York: Basic Books, 1997. A brief history of the universe and other astronomy topics.

Moeschl, Richard. *Exploring the Sky*. Chicago: Chicago Review Press, 1993. Projects and information about the universe and other astronomy topics for beginning astronomers.

VanCleave, Janice. *Janice VanCleave's Constellations for Every Kid*. New York: Wiley, 1997. Fun, simple astronomy experiments, including information about the Milky Way and other star groups.

7

Calendars

DID YOU KNOW?

A person born on February 29 has fewer birthdays!

The first recorded observations of astronomers indicate that they followed the cycles of motion of the Sun and the phases of the Moon. **Phases** are the regularly recurring changes in shape of the lighted part of a celestial body, such as a planet or the Moon, facing Earth. One cycle of Moon phases takes about 29½ days. These early observers knew that the Sun appeared to process steadily westward during the day, and that the Moon's phases changed form **new moon,** when the side of the Moon facing Earth is not fully lighted, to

full moon, when the side of the Moon facing Earth is fully lighted, then back to new moon during one cycle. But they did not realize that these events were the result of the motions of the Earth and the Moon.

By keeping records, early astronomers were able to use the motions of the celestial bodies to keep time. The records they kept became the first calendar. A **calendar** is a system for **reckoning** (counted or calculated) time by dividing it into days, weeks, months, and years. A **day** is the time it takes the Earth to make one rotation on its **axis** (an imaginary line through the center of a body that the body rotates about). In the past, a day was the period of time from sunrise to sunset, but today it is from midnight to midnight and is called a **solar day.** The ancient Egyptians in the fourth century B.C. were the first people known to divide the day into 24 equal parts. Today we call these parts **hours.**

A **year** is the time it takes the Earth to **revolve** (orbit) about the Sun and is called a **solar year** or **seasonal year.** The length of a solar year is about 365¼ days. Ancient peoples didn't realize that Earth revolved around the Sun, but their year was about 365 days because they based it on the seasons. For example, a year was reckoned from one spring to the next.

The first calendar was based on the **lunar month,** which is the time from one new moon to the next. The length of a lunar month is about 29½ days. The problem of having half a day was solved by having one month with 29 days and the next with 30, followed by one with 29, and so on.

One problem with the lunar calendar was that it did not correspond with the solar year. Twelve lunar months are about 354 days, but a solar year is about 365¼ days. This means that spring would not start on the same day each year. Over time, the first day of spring would not even occur in the same season.

In 46 B.C. the Roman statesman Julius Caesar (100–44 B.C.) reformed the calendar and based it on the solar year. This calendar, known as the **Julian calendar,** fixed the normal year at 365 days. The Julian calendar also established the order of the months and the days of the week as they exist in present-day calendars. A **week** is a seven-day time period based on the Judeo-Christian tradition of resting on the seventh day.

Since a solar year is not exactly 365¼ days long but 365 days, 5 hours, 48 minutes, and 45 seconds, the Julian calendar was 11 minutes and 15 seconds short. This extra time added up, and by 1582 the **vernal equinox** (first day of spring), which usually occurs on or about March 21, occurred 10 days early. This meant that church holidays did not occur in the appropriate seasons. Pope Gregory XIII issued a decree dropping 10 days from the calendar. To prevent the problem from happening again, he established a new calendar, know as the **Gregorian calendar.** This calendar was basically the Julian calendar, but the solution for the extra quarter day each year was to have what is called a **leap year** every fourth year, to which an extra day was added. Century years divisible evenly by 400 would be leap years, and all other century years would be common years. Thus, 1600 was a leap year, but 1700 and 1800 were common years.

The Gregorian calendar is still in use today and can be calculated for any year in advance. Today, the extra day in leap years is added in February. During a leap year there are 29 days in February instead of the normal 28 days. So an 80-year-old person whose birth day is February 29 would have celebrated only 20 birthdays on his or her actual birth date.

FUN TIME!

Purpose

To construct a calendar for one lunar month.

Materials

sheet of typing paper
pen
ruler

Procedure

1. Use the paper, pen, and ruler to draw a calendar of 5 weeks as shown.

2. Fill in the dates on the calendar, starting with the day you prepare the calendar. The calendar may include parts of 2 months.

Sun.	Mon.	Tues.	Wed.	Thur.	Fri.	Sat.

3. Observe the shape of the Moon for 29 days. Draw the shape of the Moon for each day on the calendar. Check the weather report in the newspaper or on television for the time of moonrise. The Moon rises about 50 minutes later each day. For half of the month, the Moon rises during the daytime.

Results

You have made a lunar calendar for one month. The apparent shape of the Moon changes.

Why?

The changes in the Moon's apparent shape are called phases. Phases are seen because the Moon revolves around Earth. As it revolves, different amounts of the side of the Moon facing Earth are lighted by the Sun. During the new moon phase, the Moon is between Earth and the Sun. The side of the Moon facing the Sun is lighted, so the side facing Earth is dark. As the Moon moves in its orbit, more and more of the side facing Earth is lighted.

A few days after new moon, a small amount of the Moon is lighted. This occurs on the right side of the Moon in the **Northern Hemisphere,** the region of Earth north of the **equator** (an imaginary line that divides Earth in half).

This lighted area, which resembles a ring segment with pointed ends, is called a **crescent.** A week later, the right half of the side facing Earth is lighted; this phase is called the **first quarter.** A few days later, more than half the Moon is lighted and is called a gibbous moon. About 2 weeks after new moon, all of the Moon facing Earth is lighted and the phase is called full moon. In the phases from new Moon to full Moon, the Moon is said to be **waxing** (increasing in quantity). Following the full Moon, the Moon goes through the same phases in reverse and the Moon is said to be

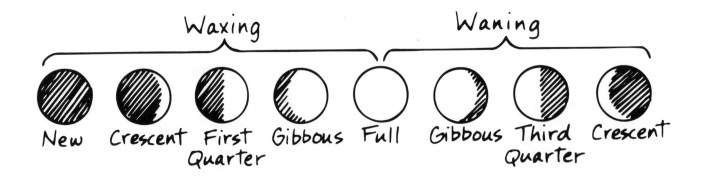

waning (decreasing in quantity). The quarter phase of the waning Moon is called the **third quarter,** and the left half of the side facing Earth is lighted.

MORE FUN WITH CALENDARS!

The Sun rises and sets in a different place along the **horizon** (the circular line that forms the boundary where the sky and Earth appear to meet) during the year. Determine the changing location of the Sun each month by viewing its position below the horizon just after sunset. *CAUTION: Do not look directly at the Sun because it can permanently damage your eyes.* To determine the Sun's location, view the sunset from the same position, such as from your bedroom window, on the first day of each month. You can make drawings of objects along the horizon as reference points. Date each drawing and compare them to predict where the Sun will set on special days, such as your birthday.

BOOK LIST

Koppeschaar, Carl. *Moon Handbook.* Chico, Calif.: Moon Publications, 1995. A guide to the Moon, including lunar calendars, geography of the Moon, and lunar travel.

Moeschl, Richard. *Exploring the Sky.* Chicago: Chicago Review Press, 1993. Projects and information about calendars and other astronomy topics for beginning astronomers.

VanCleave, *Janice. Janice VanCleave's Solar System.* New York: Wiley, 2000. Experiments about the Moon and other solar system topics. Each chapter contains ideas that can be turned into award-winning science fair projects.

Telescopes

DID YOU KNOW?

*Children may have accidentally
invented the first telescope!*

No one knows who first put together the right combination of lenses to make the first **telescope** (an instrument used to make distant objects appear nearer and larger). One story is that some children playing in an Amsterdam optical shop owned by the Dutch spectacle maker Hans Lippershey (c.1570–1619), happened to look through two lenses at the same time and saw an amazing magnified world. Another story says that Lippershey himself made the discovery. In any case, Lippershey improved on the discovery by putting two lenses in a tube, one at each end. He called the invention a "looker" and sold them in his shop.

Lippershey's "looker" was used as a telescope to view distant objects as well as a **microscope,** which is an instrument used to magnify tiny or **microscopic** (not visible to the naked eye) objects.

Others say that the Dutch spectacle maker Zacharias Janssen (1580–1638) was the inventor of both the telescope and the **compound microscope** (microscope with two or more lenses). Whoever first came up with the idea, we know that it happened some time in the early 1600s. As with many inventions, it is possible that several people independently discovered the magnifying effect of using two lenses.

Galileo, is often given credit for the invention of the telescope, as well as for being the first person to study the sky with the instrument. Galileo didn't invent the telescope, but he did make improvements. And Galileo may not have been the first to use a telescope to observe the sky, but he was the first to report astronomical discoveries made with a telescope, such as the fact that Jupiter has moons.

The first Galilean telescope was made in the summer of 1609 with a lead pipe. It had a magnification of 3×, which means it magnified things so that they looked three times nearer as when viewed with the naked eye. Galileo continued to improve and increase the magnification of his telescopes. Later Galilean models were about 30×, which was 10 times the magnification of his first model, so it made things look 30 times nearer.

Today, many telescopes use an arrangement of lenses that gathers light and forms an image of an object. An **image** is a likeness of an object. Designed in 1611 by Johanes Kepler, this instrument is called a **refracting telescope** or **Keplerian telescope.** A Keplerian telescope provides greater magnification than a Galilean telescope, but the lenses used caused images to be upside down.

In 1721, Isaac Newton improved the design of the telescope by using a combination of a mirror and a lens. This is called a **reflecting telescope** or **Newtonian telescope.** Today the largest telescope on Earth is the Keck Telescope, which is a reflecting telescope. The mirror that is pointed toward the sky and gathers light is made up of 36 mirrors, each measuring about 6 feet 7 inches (2 m) across. The Hubble Space Telescope (HST), with a light-gathering mirror about 8 feet (2.4 m) across, is a reflecting telescope that orbits the Earth. It was launched on April 25, 1990, and is used to observe distant objects in space.

FUN TIME!

Purpose

To build a simple refracting telescope.

Materials

masking tape
sheet of newspaper with some large print
2 magnifying lenses

Procedure

1. Tape the newspaper to a wall at eye level.

2. Pace off three steps from the newspaper, then turn and face the paper.

3. Close one eye and hold one of the magnifying lenses in front of your open eye.

4. Hold the second lens directly in front of the first lens.

5. Slowly move the second lens toward the newspaper until a clear image of the large print on the paper is seen.

3 paces

Results

Print on the newspaper appears enlarged and upside down.

WHY?

The image seen through the two lenses is similar to images viewed through a simple refracting telescope. The parts of a refracting telescope can be compared to the lenses in this investigation. The lens farther from the eye behaves similarly to the **objective lens** of a refracting telescope. This is the lens that faces the object being viewed and gathers the light. The objective lens produces an inverted (upside-down) image near a point within the telescope where the light rays come together, called the **focal point.** The **eyepiece,** which is the lens you look through, magnifies the image formed by the objective lens and sends this enlarged image to your eye. A reflecting telescope works in a similar way except that mirrors gather and direct the image to the focal point, where it is magnified by the eyepiece.

MORE FUN WITH TELESCOPES!

Binoculars are actually two simple telescopes that are connected. Binoculars produce upright images because they have **prisms** (solid see-through materials that change the direction of light passing through.) inside, which turn the upside-down image back upright. Use binoculars to study different celestial bodies in the nighttime sky. Try to find the moons around Jupiter or the craters on the Moon.

(To get information about the celestial bodies visible on any specific night, see an astronomy magazine, such as *Sky & Telescope.*)

BOOK LIST

Matloff, Gregory. *Telescope Power.* New York: Wiley, 1993. Information about telescopes, including fun activities and projects.

Schultz, Ron. *Looking Inside Telescopes and the Night Sky.* Santa Fe, N.M.: John Muir Publishing, 1992. Describes different kinds of telescopes, how they work, and what they tell us about the universe.

Scott, Elaine. *Close Encounters: Exploring the Universe with the Hubble Space Telescope.* New York: Disney Press, 1998. Explains what scientists have learned about our solar system and the universe from information collected by the Hubble Space Telescope.

VanCleave, Janice. *Janice VanCleave's Help! My Science Project Is Due Tomorrow!* Hoboken, N.J.: Wiley, 2002. Easy science projects, including ones about telescopes, that you can do overnight.

Planetary Motion

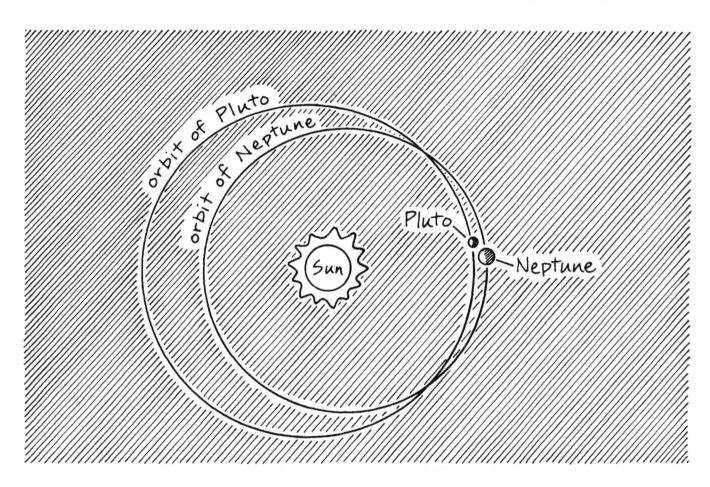

orbit of Pluto

orbit of Neptune

Sun

Pluto

Neptune

DID YOU KNOW?

Pluto is not always the farthest planet from our Sun!

Many important early ideas in astronomy were developed by Greek philosophers and scholars. Plato (c.428–c.347 B.C.), who considered circular motion to be perfect, stated that the planets orbits must therefore be circular. This was the generally accepted belief until the 1600s.

During the late 1500s, Tycho Brahe made detailed observations of planetary motion, but couldn't explain what he saw. The planets did not seem to move in completely circular orbits. Although he was concerned that someone else would use his data and not give him credit for it, he agreed to work with Johannes Kepler to get to the bottom of the mystery. Kepler had poor eyesight and was not able to make his own observations of planetary motion. But Kepler suspected that the orbits of planets are **elliptical** (oval). Kepler needed Brahe's observational data to determine the real shape of the orbits. So the thinker and the observer worked together. In 1609, after Brahe's death, Kepler published his opinion that only elliptical orbits of planets around the Sun could explain the motion that Brahe had observed.

Venus' apparent motion, unlike most planets, including Mars, Jupiter, and Saturn is not in a general east-west direction across the sky. Instead, it is seen only near the eastern and western horizons at either sunrise or sunset. Using his homemade telescopes, Galileo observed that Venus has phases like the Moon. These observations confirmed that Venus does not orbit Earth, as was commonly believed, and that Venus is closer to the Sun than Earth is.

Early models of the universe depicted the solar system with Earth at the center and Saturn as the outermost planet. The modern view of the solar system describes a group of celestial bodies orbiting the star known as the Sun, with Pluto as the outermost planet. The Sun is one of at least 100 billion known stars in our Milky Way Galaxy, and this galaxy is just one of many in the vast universe. (See chapter 6 for more on the universe.)

A **satellite** is a body that orbits a planet or star (a sun). **Natural satellites** are celestial bodies that orbit a planet or star. The natural satellites orbiting the Sun include **asteroids** (small irregular bodies also called minor planets) and nine major planets; in order from the Sun, Mercury, Venus, Earth, Mars, Jupiter, Saturn, Uranus, Neptune, and Pluto. Natural satellites that orbit planets, include moons or particles that makeup rings. Man-made bodies boosted into orbits, such as around Earth are called **artificial satellites.** Uranus was discovered by the German-born British astronomer Sir William Herschel (1738–1822) in 1781. Neptune was discovered by the English astronomer and mathematician John Couch Adams (1819–1892) in 1843. The discovery of

Pluto was mathematically predicted by the American astronomer Percival Lowell (1855–1916) in 1905. American astronomer Clyde William Tombaugh (1906–1997) discovered Pluto in 1930.

The new larger and more powerful modern telescopes, some of which have been placed on Earth-orbiting spacecraft, provide more accurate observations of planetary motion. With these instruments, astronomers have determined that the planets' orbits lie within each other except for those of the outer two planets, Neptune and Pluto. Neptune's orbit extends farther from the Sun at one end making Neptune, not Pluto, the farthest planet from the Sun for about 20 years. This last happened between January 21, 1979, and March 14, 1999, and will not occur again until September 2226.

FUN TIME!

Purpose

To determine why Neptune and Pluto do not crash into each other where their orbits overlap.

Materials

12-inch (30-cm) –square piece of poster board
scissors
drawing compass
ruler
pencil
marker
transparent tape

Procedure

1. Fold the piece of poster board in half and cut it along the fold.

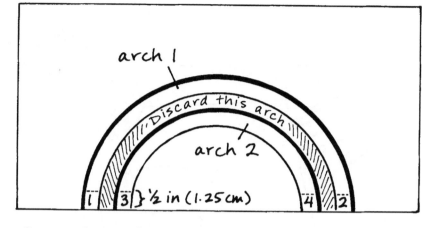

arch 1

Discard this arch

arch 2

1 3 } ½ in (1.25 cm) 4 2

2. On one piece of the poster board, use the compass to draw four semicircles with these diameters: 8 inches (20 cm), 7 inches (17.5 cm), 6 inches (15 cm), and 5 inches (12.5 cm).

3. Use the pencil to draw two ½-inch (1.25-cm) tabs across the bottom of the outer and inner arches (arches 1 and 2) as shown. With the marker, color a narrow band on the outside of arches 1 and 2. Label the tabs and arches.

4. Cut out arches 1 and 2, discarding the arch that separates them.

5. Stand arch 1 across the center of the second piece of poster board by bending the tabs on the arch and taping them to the poster board as shown.

6. Draw a sun on the poster board between the tabs and about 2½ inches (7.5 cm) from the end of tab 1.

7. Stand arch 2 by bending tab 3 and placing it at an angle to arch 1 as shown. Tape tab 3 in place.

8. Bend tab 4 and tape it to the poster board so that it is in line with tab 3.

Results

The two arches overlap but do not touch each other.

Why?

Most of the time Pluto is the farthest planet from the Sun. But at times Neptune's orbit

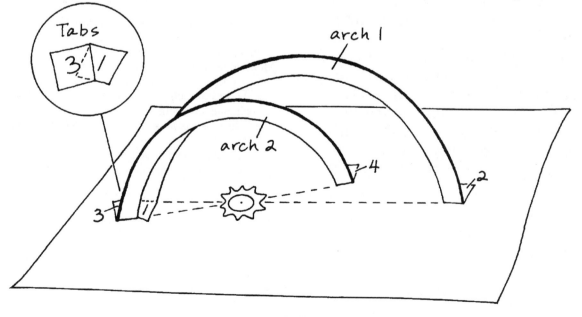

Tabs

3 1

arch 1

arch 2

3 1 4 2

(represented by arch 2) crosses Pluto's orbit (arch 1). At those times, one end of Pluto's orbit (tab 1) is closer to the Sun than is Neptune's orbit (tab 3), placing Neptune farther from the Sun. Because the orbits of these two planets are at an angle of about 16° to each other and never closer than 240,000,000 miles (384,000,000 km), there is no danger of the planets colliding.

MORE FUN WITH ORBITS!

While a circle has one center point, an **ellipse** (oval shape) has two **foci** (points in line with each other and on either side of the center point of the ellipse). For a planet, the Sun is located at one focus, and nothing is at the other focus. Draw the shape of a planet's elliptical orbit by using a pen to mark a dot in the center of a 10-inch (25-cm) –square piece of poster board. Label the dot "Sun" and draw rays around the dot. Draw a second dot 2 inches (5 cm) away from the first dot. Ask an adult to use a pencil to make a hole through each dot on the poster board. Insert a paper brad in each of the holes and secure the brads. Tie the ends of an 8-inch (20-cm) piece of string together to form a loop, then place the loop around the brads. Place the point of the pencil against the inside of the loop, and with the string taut and the pencil's point against the paper, move the pencil around inside the loop until it is back at the starting

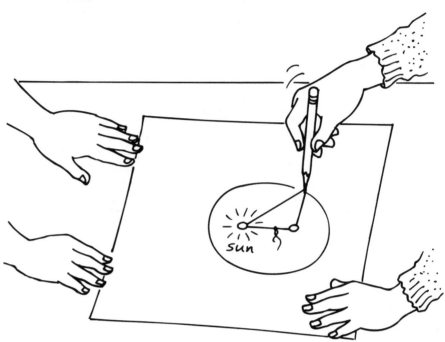

point. In a planet's orbit, the point closest to the Sun is called **perihelion** and the point farthest from the Sun is called **aphelion.** (In the figure, as well as in your drawing for this investigation, the orbit drawn is more elongated than any of the planets' orbits.)

BOOK LIST

Filkin, David. *Stephen Hawking's Universe.* New York: Basic Books, 1997. A brief history of the cosmos and other astronomy topics, including planetary motion.

Moeschl, Richard. *Exploring the Sky.* Chicago: Chicago Review Press, 1993. Projects and information about the discovery and orbits of each planet and other astronomy topics for beginning astronomers.

VanCleave, Janice. *Janice VanCleave's Solar System.* New York: Wiley, 2000. Experiments about planetary motion and other solar system topics. Each chapter contains ideas that can be turned into award-winning science fair projects.

10 Gravity

DID YOU KNOW?

You can be weightless without going into space!

Throughout history many attempts have been made to explain gravity. In the fourth century B.C., Aristotle claimed that the Earth was made of four elements—earth, air, fire, and water—which had their natural places and toward which they tended to travel. He taught that heavier objects containing greater amounts of earth than others would fall toward Earth faster. Galileo had a different view, which was that gravity causes all things to fall at the same acceleration. **Acceleration** is a change or increase in speed, and Galileo correctly believed that every falling object's speed changed at the same rate. Legend has it that Galileo demonstrated his ideas about gravity to his students by dropping a cannonball and a smaller musket ball from the Leaning Tower of Pisa, and the balls hit the ground at the same time.

Sir Isaac Newton used the information from Galileo's work to describe the force of gravity and the motion of objects throughout the universe. According to another legend, an apple fell on Newton's head when he was sitting under an apple tree, and this started him thinking about falling things. The apple fell because of a force called gravity. Weight is the measure of gravity and one unit of weight is the newton (N), named in honor of Sir Isaac Newton.

Falling apples, people, or any other objects in free fall seem to be weightless. A **free fall** is the fall of an object in which gravity is the only force pulling it down. Since **weight** is a measure of the gravitational force on an object, objects in Earth's gravitational field are never weightless. But since a scale under the feet of a falling person, such as a person jumping on a trampoline, would also be falling at the same rate, the person's feet would not be pushing against the scale, and the person would have an apparent zero weight shown on the scale.

The German-born American physicist Albert Einstein (1879–1955) realized that free fall is an important clue to gravity. Einstein's thoughts were the foundation of the Reduced-Gravity Program operated by the NASA Lyndon B. Johnson Space Center in Houston, Texas. This program was started in 1959 to test the effects of microgravity environments on humans, equipment, and experimental investigations, such as the motion of objects. (A **microgravity environment** is one in which an object's apparent weight is small compared to its actual weight due to gravity.) Today, experiments in microgravity environments can be performed aboard special airplanes that fly at specific speeds and paths to produce apparent weightless periods of about 25 seconds.

The mass and size of a planet affect the strength of its gravity (g). **Surface gravity** is gravity at or near the surface of a celestial body. The **gravity rate (G.R.)** of a celestial body is its surface gravity divided by Earth's. Earth's G.R. is arbitrarily given a value of 1 g. The planets with a gravity rate less than 1 g are Mercury, Venus, Mars, Uranus, and Pluto. The remaining planets—Jupiter, Saturn, and Neptune—have a gravity rate of more than 1 g. On July 20, 1969, astronauts Neil Armstrong (b.1930) and Edwin Eugene ("Buzz") Aldrin (b.1930) stood on Earth's Moon. They were seen via satellite communication to leap around as if on trampolines due to the Moon's gravity of ⅙ g.

FUN TIME!

Purpose

To determine your weight in newtons on different planets.

Materials

bathroom scale
calculator
pencil and paper

Procedure

1. Determine your weight in pounds by weighing yourself on the scale.

2. Calculate your weight in newtons (N) by using the calculator to multiply your weight in pounds by 4.5. For example, if you weigh 90 pounds, your weight in newtons would be:

$$90 \text{ pounds} \times 4.5 = 405 \text{ N}$$

Record your weight on Earth in newtons in a weight data table like the one shown.

3. Determine and record in your Weight Data table what your weight would be on the different planets. Do this by using the calculator to multiply each planet's gravity rate listed in the table by your weight on Earth. For example, if you weigh 405 N on Earth, your weight on Mercury, which has a gravity rate of 0.38, would be:

$$0.38 \times 405 \text{ N} = 153.9 \text{ N}$$

Results

Your weight will vary on each planet. You would weigh the least on Pluto and the most on Jupiter.

Why?

Your weight is a measure of the force of gravity, which on Earth is the force with which Earth's surface gravity pulls on an object. Earth's gravity rate equals 1. Celestial bodies with a gravity rate greater than 1 have a surface gravity greater than that of Earth. Those with a gravity rate less than 1 have a surface gravity less than that of Earth. As shown in this investigation, your weight on each planet is calculated as the product of your weight on Earth times the gravity rate of each planet. The **newton** (N) is the SI unit of weight; the **pound** is the English unit of weight. Weight on celestial bodies in this investigation is measured in newtons.

		Weight Data	
Planet	**Gravity Rate (G.R.)**	**Weight on Earth in Newtons (N)**	**Weight on Planet in Newtons (G.R. × Weight on Earth)**
Mercury	0.38	405	153.9
Venus	0.91	405	
Mars	0.38	405	
Jupiter	2.54	405	
Saturn	1.16	405	
Uranus	0.91	405	
Neptune	1.19	405	
Pluto	0.06	405	

MORE FUN WITH GRAVITY!

Your apparent weight increases when you ride up in an accelerating elevator and decreases when you ride down. Investigate this for yourself by placing a bathroom scale on the floor of an elevator car. Stand on the scale and observe your weight when the elevator car is stationary. This will be your normal weight, which is equal to the force of gravity on your body. As the elevator car accelerates on the way up, the mass of your body doesn't change but your apparent weight on the scale does. This is because while you are being pulled down against the scale by gravity, the elevator car is pushing back with more force because it is accelerating upward. As the elevator car accelerates on the way down, you are being pulled against the scale by gravity, but the scale is moving away from you so your apparent weight decreases. In free fall, you and the scale would be moving at the same rate and your apparent weight would be zero.

BOOK LIST

Couper, Heather, and Nigel Henbest. *How the Universe Works.* Pleasantville, N.Y.: Reader's Digest Association, 1994. Interesting facts and activities about gravity and other astronomy topics.

Filkin, David. *Stephen Hawking's Universe.* New York: Basic Books, 1997. A brief history of the cosmos and other astronomy topics, including gravity.

Gilbert, Harry, and Diana Gilbert Smith. *Gravity, the Glue of the Universe.* Englewood, Colo.: Teacher Ideas Press, 1997. History of and activities about gravity.

VanCleave, Janice. *Janice VanCleave's Gravity.* New York: Wiley, 1993. Experiments about weightlessness and other gravity topics. Each chapter contains ideas that can be turned into award-winning science fair projects.

III

BIOLOGY

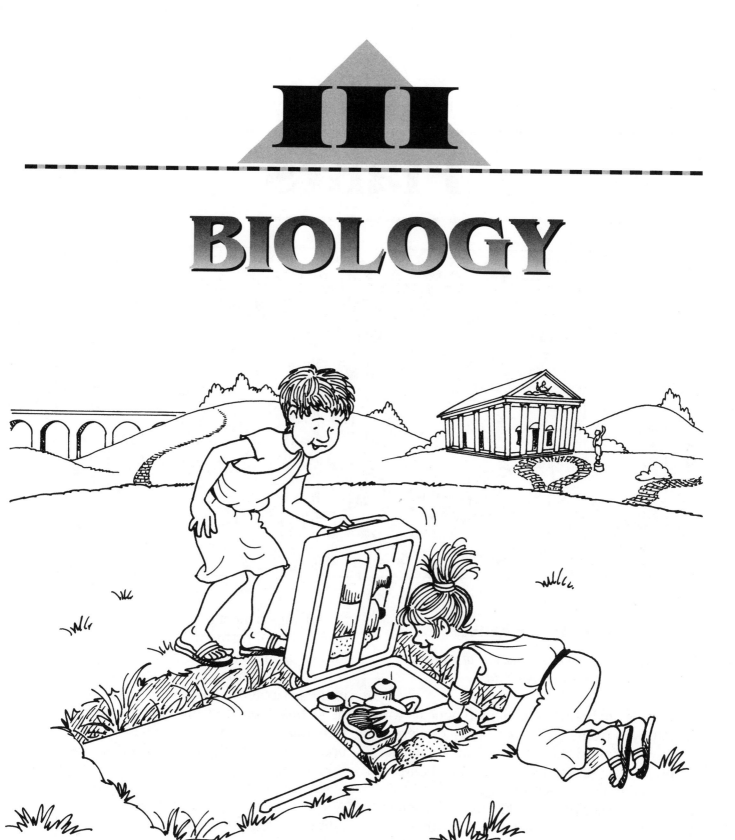

Plants

DID YOU KNOW?

*A forest "sweats" thousands of gallons
of water each day!*

Botany is the branch of biology that deals with the study of plants. Prehistoric peoples were mainly interested in how plants and animals could be used for food, clothing, and shelter. Most of the botany and **zoology** (the study of animals) studies prior to 500 B.C. were confined to using plants and animals **medicinally** (for their healing properties) and **agriculturally** (in farming) uses. Ancient peoples did not know that willow bark contained salicylic acid, a substance used today to make aspirin, but they used the bark to reduce fever and pain.

Aristotle's most famous pupil, the Greek scientist Theophrastus (c.372–c.287 B.C.), is known as the father of botany. When Aristotle retired, Theophrastus succeeded him as head of the peripatetic school in the Lyceum, where he lectured for 35 years. Theophrastus is most remembered for his books on plants, which presented the first thorough treatment of the science of botany and remained the authoritative opinion on the subject through the Middle Ages (c.500–c.1500). The views of Theophrastus—right or wrong—were accepted in Europe without serious question for almost 2,000 years. Interest in science in general declined during the Middle Ages, but was reborn in the fifteenth century due in part to explorers such as Christopher Columbus

(1451–1506), who brought back to Spain new plants from the New World.

Exploration of the microscopic world began in the early seventeenth century when the compound microscope was invented. The microscopic studies of plants in the seventeenth century were the start of the study of plant anatomy. The English botanist Stephen Hales (1677–1761) pioneered the study of plant **physiology** (the study of life processes). Among the processes studied by Hales were the movement of sap through plants, **photosynthesis** (the process by which plants in the presence of light make food), and **transpiration** (the process by which plants lose water through their leaves). Plants don't *really* sweat, but because of transpiration, a forest can add many hundreds of gallons of water to the air each day.

Botany studies today are carried out in the wild as well as in **botanical gardens** (areas in which plants are grown primarily for scientific studies and/or for viewing by the public). Many botanical gardens contain large **herbaria** (collections of pressed, dried plants) used as reference for classifying unknown plants.

FUN TIME!

Purpose

To demonstrate water loss by plants.

Materials

masking tape
tall slender jar
tap water
scissors
sprig from a plant with 5 or more leaves and a 6-inch (15-cm) or longer stem
cooking oil
ruler
marking pen

Procedure

1. Place a strip of tape down the side of the jar.
2. Fill the jar about three-fourths full with water.
3. With adult permission, cut a sprig from a plant. The stem of the sprig should measure 6 inches (15 cm) or longer and have five or more leaves.
4. Cut the end of the stem at an angle and stand the sprig in the jar of water. The stem does not have to touch the bottom of the jar.
5. Pour enough oil into the jar to cover the water's surface with about ¼ inch (0.63 cm) of oil.
6. With the pen, mark the height of the water in the jar on the tape.
7. Set the jar near a window that receives direct sunlight for at least part of the day.
8. Each day for 7 or more days, mark the level of the water in the jar.

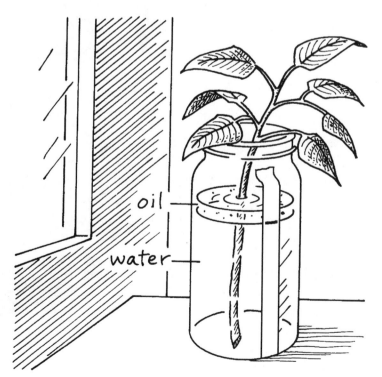

Results

The water level decreases each day.

Why?

The oil on the surface of the water prevents the water from **evaporating** (changing from a liquid to a gas), so any change in the water level is due to the water moving through the stem of the plant sprig to the leaves and then out of the leaves through holes called **stomata** as water **vapor** (a gas formed from a substance that is usually a solid or a liquid at room temperature). This is the process of transpiration discovered by Stephen Hales. A large amount of the water in the air comes from plants.

MORE FUN WITH LEAVES!

Make your own leaf herbarium. Do this by collecting whole leaves. Place the leaves between two sheets of construction paper. Sandwich the papers between sheets of newspaper and press them between two heavy books. After 2 weeks, the leaves should be flat and dry. If not, press them for a longer time. Use very small pieces of transparent tape to secure the leaves to the construction paper. Write information about each leaf on the paper, such as where and when you found it and the type of plant it came from. Place the papers in a binder for safe keeping.

BOOK LIST

Braithwaite, Althea. *Trees and Leaves*. New York: Troll Associates, 1990. Information about trees, including transpiration and how to identify trees from their leaves.

VanCleave, Janice. *Janice VanCleave's Plants*. New York: Wiley, 1997. Experiments about leaves, transpiration, and other plant topics. Each chapter contains ideas that can be turned into award-winning science fair projects.

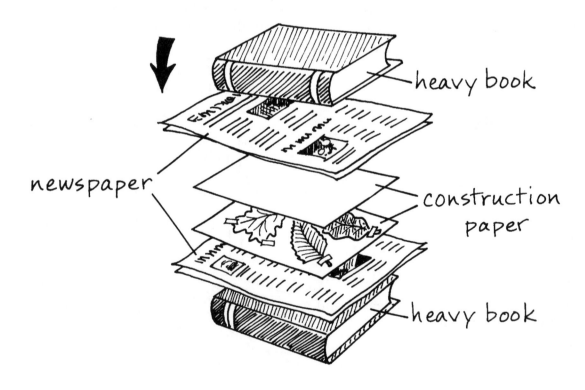

newspaper — heavy book — construction paper — heavy book

Anatomy

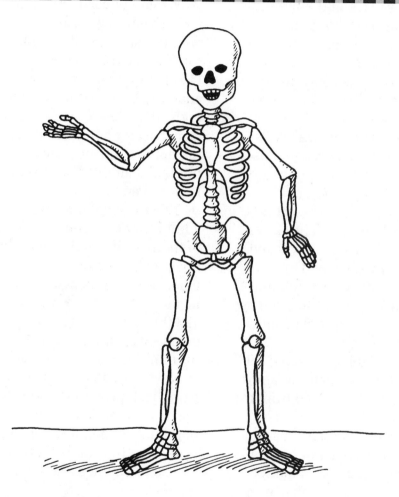

DID YOU KNOW?

Ancient skeletons communicate!

Anatomy is the study of the structure of organisms. Human anatomy is the study of the human body, including everything from the skeletal framework to skin and hair. (The **skeleton** is a structural frame work made of bone that supports the body and allows it to move.) The ancient Egyptians around 3000 B.C., who embalmed the bodies of the dead, often first removing parts such as the heart and other organs, certainly knew something about the structure of the human body. But some of the first written recorded studies of anatomy were made by ancient Greeks, including the physician Hippocrates (c.460–c.377 B.C.) and the philosopher Aristotle.

For many years, religious and/or superstitious views kept people from **dissecting** (cutting apart) dead human bodies. Instead, animals were dissected and their body parts were assumed to be like body parts in the human body. Some comparisons were correct. Others total incorrect. Both Hippocrates and Aristotle believed that the human heart was where thinking took place. Not only do we now know that thinking takes place in the brain, but scientists have discovered that different thought processes occur on different sides of the brain. It is said that a person with scientific, math, and reasoning skills is mostly left-brained because this is the side of the brain where those thought processes occur. A person with creative, artistic, and musical skills would be mostly right-brained, because these processes occur on that side of the brain.

Soon after the death of Aristotle, the Greeks began to allow occasional dissections of human cadavers (dead bodies). The Greek physicians Herophilus (c.335–c.280 B.C.) and Erasistratus (fl.c.250 B.C.) performed many dissections. Herophilus proved that thinking takes place not in the heart but in the brain. Erasistratus traced nerves to the brain, and veins and arteries to the heart.

The Greek physician Galen (A.D. 129–c.199) wrote 500 books about human anatomy, a few of which still exist. His facts, obtained from the dissection of animals, turned out to contain many errors when applied to human anatomy. Nevertheless, he was accurate about many things, including the identification of numerous muscles and the function of many nerves. he insisted, however, that tiny pores existed in the heart through which blood passed from the right side to the left. His errors were accepted throughout Europe for more than 1,000 years.

An unlikely anatomist was the Italian artist, Leonardo da Vinci (1452–1519). In his time , he was admired chiefly for his art and art theory. His interest in science, including anatomy, is a modern discovery. Leonardo illegally dissected human cadavers and made over 700 detailed drawings of the human body, including the skeleton. Leonardo's notes were written in a peculiar right-to-left script that could be read with a mirror.

While Leonardo most likely discovered that Galen's views were not all true, his work was not published. So it was not until 1543, when the Flemish physician Andreas Vesalius (1514–1564) published the first book on anatomy based on dissections of the human body, that Galen's views were replaced with facts based on human dissections. Because of his many contributions to the understanding of human anatomy, Vesalius is known as the father of anatomy.

Even ancient anatomists knew that the adult human skeleton consists of 206 bones, 22 of them in the skull alone. While skeletons do not speak, today we know that bones give clues to the presence of different diseases. In fact scientist have found skeletons more than 12,000 years old that show evidence of tuberculosis and other diseases. The 9,400-year-old mummified remains of Spirit Cave man, found in Nevada in 1940, indicate that he suffered from back problems and tooth abscesses. It has also been determined that with age, some of the more than 300 bones of a baby **bond** (link together) and all grow and get harder. By age 20 to 25 the skeleton has 206 hardened bones.

Histology is the microscopic study of animal and plant parts. Histology began in the seventeenth century, with improvements in the microscope. But histology progressed slowly until the nineteenth century. Today, surgeons can do microsurgery on people. The surgeon views the site through a special microscope and uses computer-controlled robotic hands to operate tiny surgical instruments.

FUN TIME!

Purpose

To determine how the shape of a bone adds strength.

materials

2 index cards
transparent tape
3 to 5 books of equal size

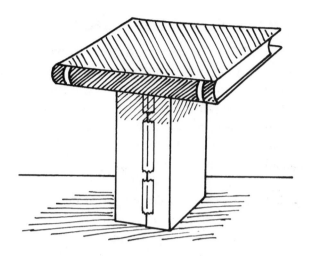

Procedure

1. Fold over about ½ inch (1.25 cm) of the short end of one of the index cards to make a tab.

2. Fold the remaining part of the card in half twice, then unfold the card to form four creases.

3. Refold the card along the creases. Then overlap the tab and secure it with tape to make a square tube. (A square is an object having four equal sides.)

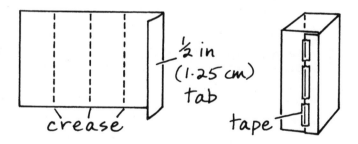

4. Stand the square tube on a table and place one of the books on top of the tube. If the tube continues to stand, add additional books one at a time until the tube collapses. Mentally note how many books the tube was able to hold.

5. Overlap the short ends of the remaining card and secure them with tape to make a **cylinder** (a object shaped like a can).

6. Repeat step 4 using the cylindrical tube.

Results

The cylindrical tube is able to hold more books.

Why?

Books are added until the weight of the books causes the tubes to collapse. If the books are positioned so that their weight pushes straight down, then both shapes will support the same number of books. But if the weight of the books is uneven, the tubes receive a sideward force. The flat walls of the **square** (four equal sides) tube are more likely to bend from a sideward force. This is because the square tube has some stronger and some weaker parts. The curved wall of the **cylindrical** (can shaped) tube basically has equal strength in all directions, so it is less likely to bend from a sideward force. Long thigh bones are hollow and relatively cylindrical in shape. This shape, like the cylindrical tube, gives these bones strength. Being hollow makes them lightweight.

MORE FUN WITH ANATOMY!

You can bend your neck and body as well as turn around because your **spine** (backbone) is made up of many separate bones. Demonstrate the effect of having a solid spine as compared to having one made of separate bones by threading a 24-inch (60 cm) piece of colored string through a straight straw. (If a flexible straw is used, cut off the short flexible end.) The string represents your **spinal cord,** which is a bundle of **nerves** (fibers that send messages form the body to and from the brain) running through the center of the spine. Holding the ends of the string, try to bend the straw. Note how hard or easy it is to bend the straw. Remove the straw and cut it into eight or more pieces. These pieces represent the short bones in your spine called **vertebrae.** Thread the string through each piece of straw. Again holding the ends of the string, try to bend the straw and note how easily it bends.

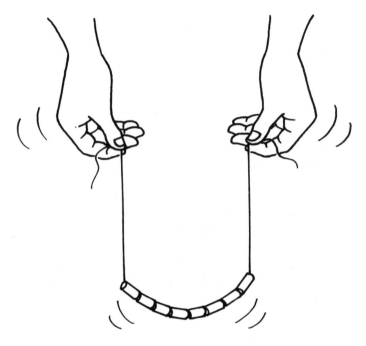

BOOK LIST

Bender, Lionel. *Human Body.* New York: Crescent Books, 1992. Interesting fact about the human body, including historical achievements of various scientists.

Parker, Steve. *How the Body Works.* Pleasantville, N.Y.: Reader's Digest Association, 1994. Interesting facts and activities about the amazing machine that is the human body.

VanCleave, Janice. *Janice VanCleave's The Human Body for Every Kid.* New York: Wiley, 1995. Fun, simple human body experiments, including information about bones.

Circulatory System

ROADWAY TO HEART 1000 miles

PUMP

DID YOU KNOW?

Your body contains thousands of miles of blood vessels!

The **circulatory system** of humans is a closed network of parts including the **heart,** which pumps blood through tubes called **blood vessels. Blood** is a liquid that carries nutrients for growth and repair to **cells** (building blocks of organisms) and carries wastes away from cells. The ancient Greeks believed that the human heart was where thinking took place, and that the blood vessels contained air. The ancient Chinese believed the rhythm of the heartbeat was the key to understanding all human ailments.

The Greek physician Erasistratus thoroughly studied the circulatory system of cadavers, but saw nothing to disprove the idea that the blood vessels, now called **arteries,** carried air away from the heart. Actually, arteries carry oxygen-rich blood away from the heart, but this blood is emptied into other blood vessels called **veins** (blood vessels that carry oxygen-poor blood back to the heart) and **capillaries** (small blood vessels that connect arteries and veins). The arteries of cadavers are empty of blood.

The English physician William Harvey (1578–1657) was the first to discover how blood circulates. He was not the first to suggest some form of closed circulatory system, but he was the first to work out some of the details of its motion from the heart through one kind of vessel (arteries) and back through another kind of vessel (veins). He suggested that thousands of miles of tiny invisible blood vessels (capillaries) connect veins and arteries. With the aid of a microscope, Harvey's beliefs were confirmed by the Italian biologist Marcello Malpighi (1628–1694). We now know that there are capillary links between capillaries and veins and arteries called **venules** and **arterioles,** respectively.

Studies of the blood by the Dutch biologist Jan Swammerdam (1637–1680) revealed **red blood cells** (cells in blood that transport oxygen). Today it is known that red blood cells are red because of **hemoglobin,** a chemical that is responsible for the ability of these cells to transport oxygen from the lungs to every part of the body. The Austrian-born American scientist Karl Landsteiner (1868–1943) discovered the four major blood types (A, B, AB, and O), paving the way for the safe use of blood transfusions. Later the American physician Charles Richard Drew (1904–1950) discovered that **plasma** (the liquid part of blood), unlike whole blood, could be stored for a long time when refrigerated. He also found that, whereas whole blood had to match each person's specific blood type plasma could be used by anyone. In 1942, Drew patented a device that improved the process of preserving blood.

On December 3, 1967, South African physician Christiaan Barnard (b.1922) performed the first successful heart transplant surgery, but the patient died 18 days later. In 1969, American physician Denton Arthur Cooley (b.1920) was the first surgeon to implant a temporary artificial heart in a patient. The patient was kept alive with this heart for 65 hours, until a real heart could be located and used. The first permanent artificial heart was implanted in a human being in December 1982. The patient lived for 112 days. On July 3, 2001 in Louisville, Kentucky, the heart of an American male, Robert Tools (1942–2001), was replaced with a mechanical heart. Robert died November 30, 2001 from health problems not associated with the heart. At this time the mechanical heart may extend the life of some patients until a heart transplant can be done. In the future a mechanical heart may be the final replacement for those needing a new heart.

FUN TIME!
Purpose

To identify blood vessels.

Materials

flashlight
hand mirror

Procedure

1. Raise your tongue and shine the light on the area under the tongue.

2. Use the mirror to inspect the area under your tongue.

3. Find the blood vessels identified in the drawing.

- capillary links—hair-thin red and bluish red blood vessels that connect veins and arteries to capillaries
- veins—large blue blood vessels

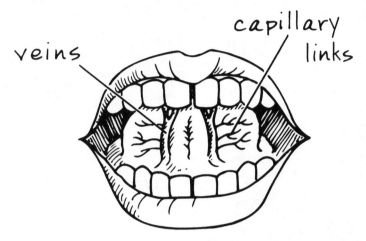

Results

Large blue vessels and hair-thin red and bluish red vessels are seen under the tongue.

Why?

The main blood vessels in the circulatory system are arteries, veins, and capillaries. Large blue veins carrying blue, oxygen-poor blood back to the heart are often seen beneath the skin. Arteries are also large vessels, but because they are generally not near the skin, they are not usually seen. Capillaries connected to veins contain bluish red oxygen-poor blood. Capillary links are the venules and arterioles that connect the ends of veins and arteries to capillaries. Veins and capillary links can be seen under the tongue.

MORE FUN WITH THE CIRCULATORY SYSTEM!

Each time your heart **contracts** (draws together), blood is forced through the arteries. The blood moves at a rhythmic rate, causing the arteries to pulsate, or throb. An artery lies close to the skin in the wrist, so the heartbeat, or **pulse,** can be felt and counted. Do this by laying your arm on a table with the palm of your hand up. Place the fingertips of your other hand on your upturned wrist below the thumb. Gently press until you can feel your heartbeat. You may have to move your fingertips around the area until you feel your heartbeat. Count the number of heartbeats that you feel in one minute, or count the heartbeats in 30 seconds and multiply by 2.

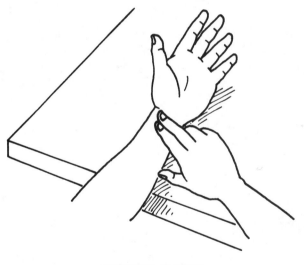

BOOK LIST

Bruun, Ruth Dowling. *The Human Body.* New York: Random House, 1982. Explains how the circulatory systems and other body parts work.

Parker, Steve. *How the Body Works.* Pleasantville, N.Y.: Reader's Digest Association, 1994. Interesting facts and activities about the amazing machine that is the human body.

VanCleave, Janice. *Janice VanCleave's The Human Body for Every Kid.* New York: Wiley, 1995. Fun, simple human body experiments, including information about circulation.

14

Preserving Food

DID YOU KNOW?

The first refrigerator was a straw-lined pit!

Preserving food is an age-old practice. Prehistoric people dried food in the Sun because someone accidentally discovered that dried food didn't spoil as quickly as fresh food. They did not know that they were producing an unacceptably dry environment for the microbes that make food go bad. **Microbes** are organisms, visible only under a microscope. Some foods are still preserved by drying, such as beef jerky (dehydrated beef) and raisins (dehydrated grapes).

Salting is another traditional method of preserving foods that is still widely used today. Salting kills some microbes that would otherwise cause meat and vegetables to go bad.

Corned beef, anchovies, and cabbage are all preserved with salt. One of the chemical parts of salt is the element sodium. Thus, one of the downsides is that these foods are very high in sodium, which increases the risk of **hypertension** (high blood pressure) in people who have inherited a tendency for this disorder.

Chilling and freezing have also long been used in cold climates as methods of preserving food. Natural ice was the first means of **refrigeration** (a process of preserving by cooling). Since the time of the early Greeks and Romans, snow and ice were harvested in winter and stored in what were the first ice chests— pits lined with **insulating** (restricting heat flow) materials such as straw. Food was packed in the ice and snow to keep it cold and the straw slowed the melting of the ice and snow.

But snow and ice weren't always available, and inventors were encouraged to develop artificial cooling methods. Francis Bacon (1561–1626), an English philosopher known for promoting investigative experimentation, died practicing the same experimental research that he supported. He was investigating the effect of temperature on meat preservation and became chilled while gathering snow and stuffing it into a freshly butchered piece of poultry. As a result, he died of bronchitis. Different investigations about refrigeration followed Bacon's death, and the first ice-making machine was invented in 1834 by Jacob Perkins (1766–1849), an American engineer living in London. Soon the first successful refrigeration machine in the United States was developed, in 1844 by the physician John Gorrie (1803–1855).

In the 1790s the French government offered a prize of 12,000 francs for a food preservation method that could be used to feed a large, constantly moving army. Nicolas François Appert (c.1750–1841), a French cook, was inspired by this offer and began experimenting. After 14 years, he devised a method for preserving food by heating and sealing it in airtight containers, and won the prize in 1810. This method, still used today, is called **canning.** Appert had no understanding of microbes, but he observed that if he heated food and put it in glass jars sealed with a cork held in place with a wire, and heated the jars in boiling water, then the food did not spoil. Canning techniques improved quickly. By the time of the American Civil War (1861–1865), canning was a major method of food preservation and remains so today. The kinds of cans used, how they are sealed, as well as how they are heated have changed to provide ways of improving the canning process. Some people still can food at home. Glass jars and lids are used in home canning. The home canning process works because the jars of food are heated, their lids are lifted by the heated air in the jar and hot air escapes. When the jars cool, a **vacuum** (a space from which gases have been removed) is produced resulting in the lids sealing tightly and preventing air from reentering. In the absence of air, an environment that inhibits the growth of some dangerous microbes is created. Other microbes are killed by the heat.

Other modern food preservation techniques include freeze-drying and food additives. In **freeze-drying,** foods are frozen in a vacuum, then their ice crystals are **vaporized** (changed to a gas). Almost anything can be freeze-dried, but because of the cost, only a few foods are, such as coffee, camp rations, and some of the food eaten by astronauts in space.

Food additives called **preservatives** are used to maintain freshness and extend the shelf life of most packaged foods. Many are natural food substances, such as sugar, salt, ascorbic acid (vitamin C), and vitamin E.

FUN TIME!

Purpose

To demonstrate how ice preserves food.

Materials

5 ounce (150 mL) paper cup
tap water
outdoor thermometer
freezer

Procedure

1. Fill the cup half full with water.

2. Stand the thermometer in the cup.

3. Place the cup in the freezer for 2 hours or until the water in the cup freezes.

4. Remove the cup from the freezer and read the temperature on the thermometer.

5. Read the temperature every 30 minutes until the ice melts.

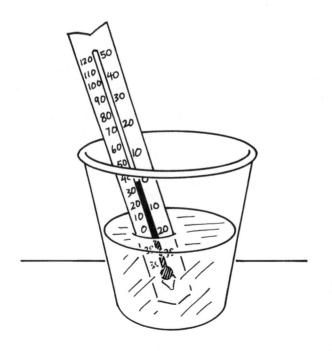

Results

The temperature remains at or below 32° F (0° C) until the ice melts.

WHY?

Ice is a good **refrigerant** (a cooling substance used in refrigeration). Ice **absorbs** (takes in) heat from warmer surroundings, cooling them while the ice warms to 32°F (0°C) and remains at this temperature until it is completely melted. Cooling stops or slows the growth of most bacteria that causes food to spoil. Cooling is a good method of preserving food.

MORE FUN WITH PRESERVING FOOD!

Pickling is a method of preserving food by which vinegar is used to kill microbes. Vinegar gives foods a sour taste. The word *pickle* is commonly used for a pickled cucumber. Make your own pickles by mixing together in a bowl ½ cup (125 mL) of apple cider vinegar, ½ cup of water (tap water works, but distilled is best), 1 teaspoon (5 mL) of salt, and 1 teaspoon (5 mL) of dried dill. Ask an adult to wash two cucumbers and cut them into slices, and then to peel and slice a small onion. Add the cucumber and onion slices to the bowl. Cover the bowl with a lid or food wrap. Place the bowl in a refrigerator for 1 day. Now you can eat your pickles.

BOOK LIST

Churchill, E. Richard. *365 More Simple Science Experiments with Everyday Materials.* New York: Black Dog & Leventhal, 1998. Easy investigations, including preserving food.

Seelig, Tina L. *Incredible Edible Science.* New York: Freeman, 1994. Fun facts and edible activities, including preserving food.

VanCleave, Janice. *Janice VanCleave's Food and Nutrition for Every Kid.* New York: Wiley, 1999. Fun, simple food experiments, including how to preserve it.

Wilkinson, Philip, and Michael Pollard. *Scientists Who Changed the World.* New York: Chelsea House, 1994. The history of different scientific discoveries and inventions, including food preservation.

Stethoscope

DID YOU KNOW?

A wooden tube was once used to help diagnose diseases!

The closing of the heart valves and the contraction of the heart muscle as they push blood through the body produce sounds that can be heard through the chest. The sounds of the heart are often described as lub-*dub*-pause-lub-*dub*-pause, and so on. Heart sounds are easily heard just by placing your ear against another person's chest. Changes in the sound of rhythm of the heart sounds can indicate health problems in a person. While there is no record of the first person to discover this fact, for centuries physicians have listened to heart sound by placing an ear against the patient's chest.

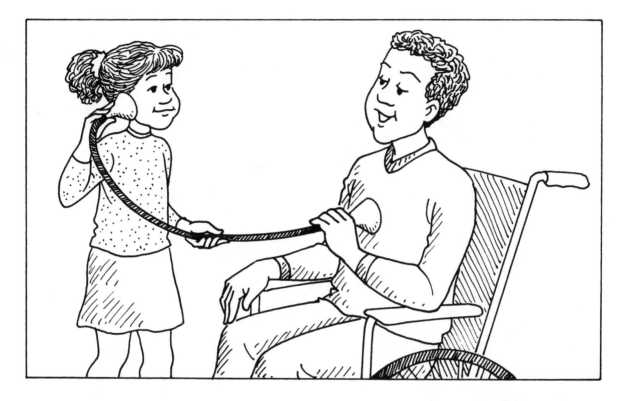

In the early 1800s, the French physician René-Théophile-Hyacinthe Laënnec (1781–1826) invented an instrument that helped physicians to better hear body sounds. This invention was the **stethoscope.** The first stethoscope was a single hollow wooden tube with a broad opening at one end, which was placed against patient's chest, and a narrow opening at the other end, which the physician placed against his or her ear.

Stethoscopes today have a flat sound receiver that is placed against the chest. The receiver is attached to two flexible rubber tubes that go in the ears. The heart sounds are clear when heard with both ears. This modern stethoscope was designed in the early 1850s by the American physician George P. Cammann (1804–1863). Stethoscopes have been improved over the years, and today some can amplify the sound so that a room full of people can hear the sounds of a patient's heart.

FUN TIME!

Purpose

To make a model of stethoscope.

Materials

knife (requires adult help)
old or inexpensive garden hose that can be cut up
2 plastic funnels large enough to fit over your ear
adult helper

Procedure

1. Ask your adult helper to cut a 3-foot (1-m) section from the garden hose, cutting across both ends of the section.

2. Firmly insert the ends of the funnels into the ends of the hose.

3. In a quiet room, ask your helper to hold one of the funnels firmly against his or her chest.

4. Place the other funnel over one of your ears.

5. Stand very still and listen to the sounds of your helper's heart.

Results

You made a stethoscope.

Why?

The funnels and hose you connected act like a stethoscope to make your helper's heart sounds louder.

MORE FUN WITH SOUNDS!

Before the stethoscope was used to listen to heart sounds, another method of using sounds to diagnose illness, called **percussion,** started around 1761. Percussion is a technique of tapping on the body, generally the chest, back, or abdomen. This method of diagnosis is still used today, and the sounds heard give clues to the size and shape of a body part inside the body. Use sounds to determine the size and shape of the inside of a closed box. Do this by taping strips of cardboard and small boxes inside school pencil boxes as shown. Number the boxes. Add one marble to each box, then tape the lids closed. Ask a helper to move box 1 back and forth to use the sounds made by the marble to draw a sketch of what he or she thinks the open space inside the box looks like. Repeat with boxes 2, 3, and 4. Open the boxes so your helper can compare his or her sketches with the contents

of the boxes. Your helper can then rearrange the cardboard strips in each box so that you can use sounds to determine the shapes of the open space inside each box.

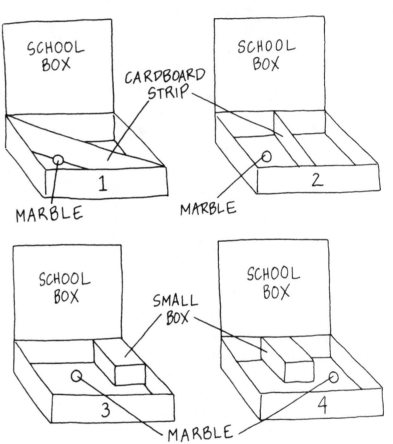

BOOK LIST

Alison, Linda. *Blood and Guts.* New York: Scholastic, 1977. Easy experiments about the human body, including information about the stethoscope.

Hurst, J. Willis. *The Heart; The Kid's Question and Answer Book.* New York: McGraw-Hill, 1998. Questions about the heart are answered by a world-renowned cardiologist.

VanCleave, Janice. *Janice VanCleave's Biology for Every Kid.* New York: Wiley, 1990. Fun, simple biology experiments, including information about the heart and its sounds.

———. *Janice VanCleave's Human Body for Every Kid.* New York: Wiley, 1995. Fun, simple body experiments, including information about the heart and its sounds.

CHEMISTRY

Chemical Reactions

DID YOU KNOW?

Chemical changes were considered magical!

Chemistry is the science that deals with the composition, structure, and properties of substances, and with the **chemical reactions** (the changing of a substance to a new substance) that these substances undergo.

In the fifth century B.C., Leucippus, a Greek philosopher, proposed that all things are made of indivisible parts. His student Democritus (c.460–c.370 B.C.) developed and popularized Leucippus's idea. These small parts were called **atoms,** from the Greek word meaning "not cut". This idea about atoms was mostly forgotten for more than 2,000 years, but the name *atom* is used today for the smallest unit of a substance, or the smallest building block of matter.

In the fourth century B.C., the Greek philosopher Aristotle promoted the idea that all materials on Earth were composed of four fundamental substances, called elements: earth, air, fire, and water. Aristotle also included on the list something called **ether,** a supposedly perfect substance of which heavenly bodies were composed.

Early explanations of chemical reactions generally involved magic. In the Middle Ages, many reactions were investigated with the prime goal of making gold. This process was called alchemy, and many scientific discoveries resulted from these early chemistry experiments. Alchemy paved the way to the publication of the first chemical textbook in 1597 with procedures for making different mixtures. (See the next chapter for more on alchemy.)

In the seventeenth century, Aristotle's ideas about elements were finally challenged. In 1661, the British chemist Robert Boyle (1627–1691) stated that only observable and weighable substances should be regarded as elements, and defined elements as the primary substances from which other substances are made. He believed that elements were composed of basic particles.

The French chemist Antoine-Laurent Lavoisier (1743–1794) is known as the founder of modern chemistry. He realized several important chemical facts, including that oxygen is needed for burning, and that substances in a chemical reaction are not created or destroyed, only changed from one form to another. This is known as the **law of conservation of matter.**

Today, **substances** are considered to be materials made of one kind of matter. Atoms are substances that cannot be broken apart by ordinary means and **molecules** are substances that can be further divided into atoms. A molecule is made of two or more atoms **bonded** (linked) together, such as oxygen (O_2). If the atoms in a molecule are of only one kind, the substance made up of these molecules is called an **element.** Not all elements are made up of

molecules, but all are made up of atoms that are alike, such as gold (Au). A **compound** is made up of a single type of molecule that contains two or more different kinds of atoms, such as water (H_2O), which contains two atoms of hydrogen for every atom of oxygen. This idea of molecules being made up of atoms was first suggested by the Italian physicist Amedeo Avogadro (1776–1856) in 1811.

The chemical composition of many millions of molecules is known today, and the number of known molecules is steadily increasing. Each molecule has a chemical name that describes its chemical content. For example, the chemical name of water (H_2O) is hydrogen oxide, which identifies its hydrogen and oxygen content. The first system of naming chemicals was presented in 1787 by a group of French chemists, including Lavoisier. This same basic system is used today.

FUN TIME!

Purpose

To demonstrate a chemical reaction.

Materials

1 teaspoon (5 mL) soil

10-ounce (300 mL) plastic glass

1 tablespoon (15 mL) 3% hydrogen peroxide (available at drugstores)

Procedure

1. Place the soil in the glass.

2. Pour the hydrogen peroxide into the glass.

3. Observe the contents of the glass periodically for 1 or more hours.

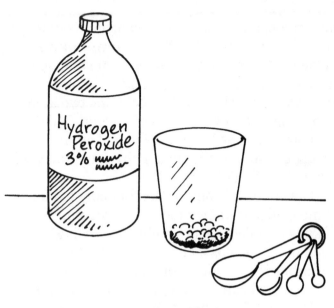

Results

Within seconds, bubbles appear on the surface of the soil. In time the bubbles stop.

Why?

An **enzyme** is a chemical found in organisms that can change the speed of a chemical reaction. Soil contains dirt, as well as parts of decayed leaves and other organisms. The remains of the living organisms contain an enzyme called catalase. Hydrogen peroxide (H_2O_2), like water, is made of hydrogen and oxygen, but in different proportions. When hydrogen peroxide **decomposes** (separates into the basic parts that make up a substance), the two parts are water (a liquid) and oxygen (a gas). In the presence of catalase, decomposition occurs quickly. The bubbles contain oxygen. When the bubbles break, the oxygen mixes with the air. When all of the hydrogen peroxide has decomposed, the bubbles stop.

MORE FUN WITH CHEMICAL REACTIONS!

A **combination chemical reaction** is one in which two or more substances combine to form one product. Demonstrate this type of reaction by first mixing 1 teaspoon (5 mL) of Epsom salts and 2 teaspoons (10 mL) of water in a paper cup. Stir this mixture until as much of the Epsom salts as possible is **dissolved** (broken up and thoroughly mixed with another substance) in the water. There may be a few undissolved salt crystals on the bottom of the cup. Add 1 tablespoon (15 mL) of liquid school glue to the cup and stir well. The product that develops is gloop.

Let the cup sit as you prepare a drying area for the gloop in the cup. Place two paper towels together, then fold the towels in half twice. Lay the folded towels in a saucer and pour the gloop in the center of the towels. Fold the towels over the gloop and press down with your fingers to squeeze out the extra liquid. Unfold the towels and use your fingers to peel the gloop off the paper. Wash and dry your hands to remove the Epsom salts, then roll the gloop into a ball in your hands. Bounce the gloop. *CAUTION: Do not eat gloop. Discard it when you're done with this experiment.*

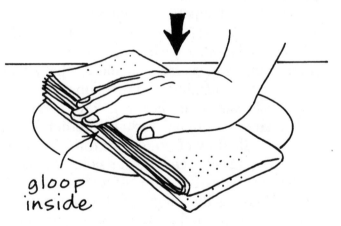

gloop inside

BOOK LIST

Marks, Diana F. *Glues, Brews, and Goos.* Englewood, Colo.: Teacher Ideas Press, 1996. Chemical recipes for different chemical reactions.

VanCleave, Janice. *Janice VanCleave's Chemistry for Every Kid.* New York: Wiley, 1989. Fun, simple chemistry experiments, including information about chemical reactions.

Alchemy

DID YOU KNOW?

Some early alchemists tried to make gold from eggs!

The Greek philosopher Aristotle taught that all matter was composed of four elements: earth, air, fire, and water. According to his theory, materials in nature were different because they contained different amounts of these four elements. Therefore, changing the ratio of the elements in a substance could transform the substance into another substance. Thus the foundation was laid for the next major phase of chemistry: alchemy.

The alchemists were at one time well respected and were often supported by kings and rulers in the hope that the alchemists would make gold for them. Of course, none of the alchemists succeeded in making gold, and those who failed sometimes lost their lives.

In their effort to make gold, some alchemists considered color and started with yellow materials, such as sulfur and even the yolk of eggs. Some considered other properties such as the fact that gold is a metal, and started with iron. Of course, silver might have been chosen, but the whole idea was to make something valuable out of something inferior, so common iron was often used as well as many other elements and compounds.

Alchemists could change some substances into others by means of what are now recognized as chemical reactions. In this way, they discovered and named the elements arsenic, antimony, bismuth, and phosphorus, among others, but they never achieved their dream of making gold.

In time, many early chemists turned their efforts from attempting to make gold toward preparing medicines. A leader in this movement was the German physician and chemist Theophrastus Bombast von Hohenheim (1493–1541), better known by his pseudonym, Philippus Aureolus Paracelsus. Paracelsus was the first chemist in Europe to mention zinc and use the word *alcohol* to refer to the content of wine.

While alchemists were not able to successfully change iron or other elements into gold by chemical reactions, scientists have learned that it is possible to do so by **nuclear reactions** (a process that produces a new element through changes in an atom's nucleus). Today chemists know that atoms such as iron and gold differ because of the number of **protons** (a positively charged particle in an atom) in their **nucleus** (center part). Iron has fewer protons than gold does, so by adding the correct number of protons to an iron atom, gold can be made. Not only is this a very costly process, but the gold would be **radioactive,** meaning it would give off a type of energy that is very dangerous to humans.

FUN TIME!

Purpose

To demonstrate how a chemical can change a metal's appearance.

Materials

white paper towel
saucer
¼ cup (63 mL) white vinegar
3 to 5 shiny pennies

Procedure

1. Fold the paper towel in half as many times as necessary so that it will fit in the bottom of the saucer.

2. Place the folded towel in the saucer.

3. Pour the vinegar in the center of the paper towel.

4. Place the pennies on top of the wet paper towel.

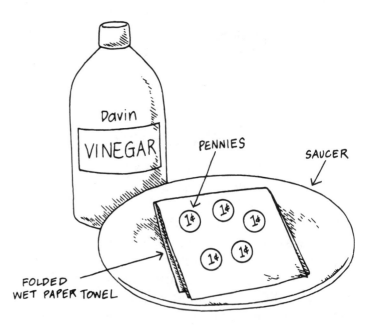

5. Note the color of the pennies and the paper towel.

6. After 24 hours, observe the color of the pennies and the paper towel again.

Results

Parts of the pennies and paper towel have turned green.

Why?

Pennies are made of bronze, a metal that contains copper. Vinegar's chemical name is acetic acid. The acetate component of acetic acid combines with the copper in the bronze pennies to produce the green coating, called copper acetate. The thin coating of green that develops on pure copper or copper alloys is called **verdigris** and can be caused by acid rain or acid gases in the air on copper such as on buildings or statues.

MORE FUN WITH ALCHEMY!

A silver-colored paper clip can be changed into a copper-colored clip. Place 10 or more pennies in a small plastic glass filled with vinegar. Hang a paper clip in the liquid by suspending it from a string tied to a pencil laid across the glass. Observe the color of the paper clip periodically for 4 or more hours. The metal clip does not change to solid copper. Instead it becomes coated with copper atoms. The copper atoms from the coins move into the vinegar and are attracted to the paper clip, to which they stick and form a thin copper-colored layer.

BOOK LIST

Did You Know. Douglas Amrine, project editor Pleasantville, N.Y.: Reader's Digest Association, 1990. Astonishing facts about hundreds of topics, including alchemy.

Hann, Judith. *How Science Works.* Pleasantville, N.Y.: Reader's Digest Association, 1991. Interesting facts and activities about alchemy and other science topics.

VanCleave, Janice. *Janice VanCleave's Chemistry for Every Kid.* New York: Wiley, 1989. Fun, simple chemistry experiments, including information about chemical reactions.

Oxidation

DID YOU KNOW?

Fire was believed to occur when an invisible substance escaped from a material!

The first fires were most likely the result of lightning. There is no record of the first time a firemaking tool was used, but objects have been found dating back thousands of years that may have been firemaking tools, including drills for producing **friction** (a force that opposes the motion of an object whose surface is in contact with another object). Friction produces heat in wood and rocks for striking sparks.

In the eighteenth century, the most popular theory about why things burned was proposed by the German chemist Georg Ernst Stahl (1660–1734). Stahl thought that materials that could burn contained an invisible substance **phlogiston.** Phlogiston (from the Greek *phlogistos,* "flammable") was believed to be a material substance that escaped when something was burned. Stahl also declared that the rusting of iron was a form of burning in which phlogiston was freed and the metal reduced to a crumbly residue called **calx**—ash.

In 1774, Joseph Priestley (1733–1804), an English clergyman, discovered oxygen and observed that things burn faster in the presence of oxygen. But instead of concluding that oxygen was needed for burning, he concluded that this invisible gas, called "new air" forced substances to give up their phlogiston more quickly.

The phlogiston theory was challenged by the French chemist Antoine Lavoisier who repeated Priestley's experiments and made further studies of the new gas. Lavoisier discovered that burning and rusting both involved oxygen, and concluded that burning and rusting result from the combination of oxygen with other substances. He also correctly recognized that the gas discovered by Priestley was a new element. In 1778, he named it oxygen.

Today, **combustion,** commonly known as **burning,** is defined as a rapid combination of a substance with oxygen accompanied by an immediate release of a significant amount of energy (such as heat). For combustion to occur, generally three things must be present: a **fuel** (a substance that will burn to produce energy), an **oxidizer** (a source of oxygen), and an **ignition stimulus** (a source of energy that will raise the fuel to the temperature at which it will catch fire). Examples of fuel are wood and paper. Air, which contains 21 percent oxygen, is the most common oxidizer. An electric spark or even another burning object, such as a match, is an ignition stimulus. **Oxidation** is the process by which oxygen combines with a substance. **Rusting** is technically the slow oxidation of any substance, with small amounts of energy given off over a period of time. But rusting is generally thought of as the oxidation of iron, producing iron oxide, a reddish brown powder commonly called **rust.**

FUN TIME!

Purpose

To show the rusting of a metal.

Materials

coarse steel wool pad (available at hardware stores)

10-ounce (300-mL) plastic glass

1 tablespoon (15 mL) vinegar

Procedure

1. Place the steel wool in the glass.

2. Pour the vinegar over the steel wool.

3. Observe the color of the steel wool immediately and then periodically for 2 or more hours.

Results

The steel wool is silvery in color at the beginning of the experiment. As time passes, parts of the steel wool have a reddish brown color.

Why?

Steel is an iron alloy. The vinegar helps the steel wool to rust by cleaning its so that the iron in the steel wool can come in contact with the oxygen in the air. The presence of the vinegar also aids in bringing oxygen in contact with the iron.

MORE FUN WITH OXIDATION

A balloon can be made to turn inside out and inflate inside a bottle as a result of rusting, which removes oxygen from the air. To demonstrate this, prepare a steel wool pad by repeating steps 1 and 2 of the original investigation. Wearing rubber gloves to protect your hands, pull the steel wool into threads and use a pencil to push them into an empty plastic soda bottle. Attach a balloon to the mouth of the bottle. Watch the balloon for 4 or more hours. The balloon appears to be sucked into the bottle. As oxygen is taken out of the air and combines with the iron in the steel wool, **air pressure** (a force that air exerts on a given area) decreases inside the bottle. Air pressure outside the bottle pushes the balloon into the bottle. Discard the bottle and its contents when you're done with this experiment.

BOOK LIST

Haven, Kendall. *Marvels of Science.* Englewood, Colo.: Librarians Unlimited, 1994. Information about 50 marvels of science, including Joseph Priestley's discovery of oxygen.

Roberts, Royston M. *Serendipity.* New York: Wiley, 1989. Accidental discoveries in science, including the discovery of oxygen.

Suplee, Curt. *Everyday Science Explained.* Washington, D.C.: National Geographic Society, 1998. Information about everyday events, including rusting.

VanCleave, Janice. *Janice VanCleave's Chemistry for Every Kid.* New York: Wiley, 1989. Fun, simple chemistry experiments, including information about oxidation.

19

Soap

DID YOU KNOW?

Early soap was made from burnt wood!

Detergent comes from the Latin word *detergere,* meaning "to clean." A **detergent** is any substance that cleans, so technically soap is a detergent. In this chapter, soap and detergent will be discussed as two separate kinds of cleaners. Soap is made from animal fat while detergents are made from chemicals derived from petroleum, but both clean in a similar way.

Soap and detergent molecules are able to clean because part of the molecule is attracted to water and another part is attracted to oil. Dirt is generally mixed with oil. Oil and water do not ordinarily mix, but soap and detergent molecules bond (link together) oil and water. Extra water then washes away the bound molecules.

Soap has been used for thousands of years, but detergents are a relatively recent discovery. Soap is thought to have been accidentally discovered when fat boiled over from a pot being heated by burning wood. **Potash,** a chemical in the wood ash, combined with the fat, producing soap. For many years the method of making soap was to put the ashes from burnt wood in a big barrel that had a small hole at the bottom. Water was then added to the barrel, and the liquid that drained out the bottom was put in a kettle with animal fat. When this mixture was cooked, the potash and fat chemically reacted, producing soap molecules that stuck together and floated to the surface of the liquid in the pot.

The earliest literary reference to soap was found on clay tablets dating from the third century B.C. in Mesopotamia. They contained a soap recipe calling for a mixture of potash and oil. In the writings of a second-century Greek physician, it was noted that cleanliness helped cure skin diseases.

For centuries, soap was made by individual homemakers. Some batches of soap came out better than others. This was because there was never any certainty as to how much potash was in the liquid that drained out of the barrels. It was not until around the nineteenth century that methods of measuring the ingredients used to make soap were developed. This made it possible to make soap with predictable results.

The type of water used can also have an effect on how well soap cleans. Water that is rich with the minerals calcium, magnesium, and/or iron is called **hard water.** Water that has few to none of these minerals is called **soft water.** The minerals that make water hard combine with the water-attracting part of the soap molecule to form a waxy solid called **soap scum,** which is **insoluble** (not able to be dissolved) in water. Soap scum leaves visible deposits on bathtubs ("bathtub ring").

The first detergent made with chemicals derived from petroleum instead of animal fat was introduced in the United States in the early 1930s. The first detergents had limited cleaning ability but were gradually improved so that instead of a single substance they were mixtures of different substances, including one having the ability to soften water. Other additives to detergents are brighteners, bleaches, perfumes, and colorants.

FUN TIME!

Purpose

To determine the effect of hard water on soap.

Materials

2 large bowls

tap water

1 tablespoon (15 mL) Epsom salts (available at drugstores)

bar of soap

towel

Procedure

1. Fill the bowls half full with water.

2. Add the Epsom salts to one of the bowls.

3. Dip your hands briefly in the bowl of plain water.

4. Hold the bar of soap in your wet hands and move the soap around to make as many suds as possible. Dip your hands in the water again if more water is needed.

5. Observe the amount of suds that were made, then rinse your hands under a faucet and dry them on the towel.

6. Repeat steps 3 to 5 using the bowl of salted water.

Results

You were able to make many suds in plain water, but hardly any in the water containing Epsom salts.

Why?

Epsom salts is a chemical that contains the mineral magnesium. Adding Epsom salts to the water makes the water hard. The soap does not make many suds when mixed with the water containing Epsom salts because the molecules of the magnesium and the fatty part of the soap bind forming soap scum.

MORE FUN WITH SOAP!

Bubble solution is a combination of soap and water molecules that bind together to form a liquid that stretches into a thin layer to surround the air blown into it thus producing a bubble. Investigate soap bubble blowing. Make a bubble solution by mixing together in a bowl 1 cup (250 mL) of water and ¼ cup (63 mL) of liquid dishwashing detergent. Cover a table with newspaper and set the bowl of bubble solution on the paper. Dip the end of a straw into the bubble solution. Remove the straw and blow into the other, dry end of the straw. How big a bubble can you blow? How many bubbles can be blown with each dip?

BOOK LIST

Churchill, E. Richard. *365 Simple Science Experiments*. New York: Black Dog & Leventhal, 1997. Easy investigations, including experiments with soap and bubbles.

VanCleave, Janice. *Janice VanCleave's 202 Oozing, Bubbling, Dripping, and Bouncing Experiments*. New York: Wiley, 1996. Fun, simple elastic experiments, and other science topics.

VanCleave, Janice. *Janice VanCleave's 203 Icy, Freezing, Frosty, Cool, and Wild Experiments*. New York: Wiley, 1999. Fun, simple experiments, including information about soap scum.

20
Dyes

DID YOU KNOW?

A royal purple dye was once made from stinky sea snails!

A **dye** is a colored substance used to color materials, such as fabrics. Dyes in a liquid solution **diffuse** (spread freely) throughout the fibers of a material. Until the mid–nineteenth century, all dyes were made from natural materials, such as leaves, twigs, roots, berries, or flowers of various plants, or from animal substances, including insects and snails. The first written record of dye use in the East was in 3000 B.C., in Chinese writings about fabrics. In western Europe, dyes are believed to have first been used around 2000 B.C. by the Swiss.

As early as 1600 B.C., the Phoenicians in Tyre extracted a purple colorant from the murex, a sea snail. The city of Tyre became famous for this dark purple dye. The dye also was known for being stinky because the snail had a garlic-like smell. It took about 20,000 snails to dye a 1-yard (1 m)–square piece of cloth, only the wealthy could afford the cloth. Many emperors through the ages wore purple, and in 424, Emperor Theodosius II of Byzantium (401–450) (now Istanbul, Turkey), issued a decree forbidding the use of certain shades of purple except by the royal family. Punishment for this offense was death.

In the fourteenth century B.C., Egyptians are believed to have first used a **mordant,** which is a chemical that fabric is soaked in to make the dye less likely to be washed out or **fade** (get lighter in color).

Woad is possibly the first plant **cultivated** (raised as a crop) for its natural dye. This plant is native to northern Europe and was used to dye fabrics. But a well-known use of the dye was by the ancient Celts, who are believed to have settled in the British Isles between the eighth and sixth centuries B.C. The story is that before battle, the British Celts painted themselves with dye from the woad plant to frighten their opponents. Around the mid–eighteenth century, another plant, indigofera, was introduced to England from India. The blue dye called **indigo** came from both indigofera and woad. A more modern use of indigo is to put the "blue" in blue jeans. As with any natural plant dye, it takes a great number of plants to extract a small amount of dye. The first **synthetic** (man-made) indigo was produced in 1880 by the German chemist Adolf von Baeyer (1835–1917). Today nearly all the world's production of indigo is synthetic rather than natural.

Natural substances remained the primary source of dye colors until the discovery of the first synthetic dye in 1856 by the English chemist Sir William Henry Perkin (1838–1907). At the age of 18, while trying to make a synthetic quinine (a medicine), Perkin discovered a bluish-purple substance that could be used as a dye. The color of this dye came to be called **mauve.** Nearly all industrial dyes used today are synthetic.

Dyes have also been used to color foods, and not just in modern times. Paintings in Egyptian tombs dating to the sixteenth century B.C. show servants preparing colored candies. The first recorded ban on food coloring was in Paris in 1396. This was a ban on the artificial coloring of butter. Ironically, in 1886 in the United States, the first approved food coloring was for butter.

After the discovery of synthetic dyes, the use of synthetic food coloring was widespread. By 1900, there were more than 690 synthetic food colorings. There was little or no control over what was added to food, and some of the colorings contained **toxic** (poisonous) substances, such as lead and mercury. In the United States in 1906, the Food and Drug Act banned the use of toxic food coloring and prohibited the use of coloring for the purpose of concealing inferiorities, such as adding red to old meats to make them look fresh. Currently, seven synthetic food colors are used. These dyes are added to only about 10 percent of foods, mostly beverages, candy and confections, pet foods, and bakery goods.

FUN TIME

Purpose

To determine the number of colorants in a candy dye.

Materials

scissors

ruler

2 round coffee filters

4 or more different colored hard candies, such as M&M's

2 cans of equal heights

large shallow cooking pan
small bowl
tap water
transparent tape

Procedure

1. Cut a 1-by-6 inch (2.5-by-15-cm) strip from the coffee filters for each candy color.

2. Set the cans in the pan and place the ruler across the cans. Space the cans as far apart as possible so that the ends of the ruler rest on their tops.

3. Fill the bowl half full with water.

4. Place one candy in the water. When the candy starts to color the water, lift the candy and shake as much water as possible off of it.

5. Rub the wet candy on a strip of paper about 1 inch (2.5 cm) from one end of the paper so that the color rubs off the candy onto the paper.

6. Tape the uncolored end of the paper to the ruler. The colored end should touch the bottom of the pan.

7. Repeat steps 4 to 6 for each candy color.

8. Allow the paper strips to dry. This should take 5 to 10 minutes.

9. Pour enough water into the pan so that the end of each paper strip just touches the water, but does not touch the color.

10. Observe the paper strips for 20 minutes or more.

Results

The colors move up the paper strip. Some of the colors separate into other colors.

Why?

Chromatography is a method of separating a mixture such as a candy dye into its different substances. In this investigation, paper was used to separate the colors in a dye that was made of a mixture of colors. Chromatography

depends on different factors, one of which is the attraction that the substances being separated have for the paper. In this investigation, the candy colors are first dissolved in water to release the dye. The dye is used to stain the paper strips. After drying, only the colorants in the dye are left in the fibers of the paper.

As the water moves through the hanging paper, the colorants dissolve in the water and move with it. The color that has the least attraction to the paper moves fastest and farthest up the paper. The other colors move slower and a shorter distance, and the one with the greatest attraction moves the slowest and the least. Some of the dyes have only one colorant and some have more. For example, green usually has blue and yellow colorants.

MORE FUN WITH DYES!

Use a coffee filter and candy dye to create a picture. To make a red flower, mold a round coffee filter over a wide-mouthed jar. Place a red candy in a bowl of water until the water starts to be colored by the candy. Shake off the excess water from the candy and use the candy to draw flower petals. Repeat this process, using more red candies to complete the flower, then use yellow candy to add a yellow center to the flower. Use green candy to make the stems and leaves. Allow the flower to dry, then stretch open the filter. You may wish to use crayons to outline your drawing and add other features to the picture, such as a Sun, clouds, birds, and so on.

BOOK LIST

Hauser, Jill Frankel. *Super Science Concoctions.* Charlotte, Vt.: Williamson Publishing, 1997. Creative science explorations, including chromatography.

Potter, Jean. *Science Arts.* Belingham, Wash.: Bright Ring Publishing, 1993. Science discoveries through art experiences, including a chromatography art project.

VanCleave, Janice. *Janice VanCleave's 203 Icy, Freezing, Frosty, Cool and Wild Experiments.* New York: Wiley, 1999. Fun, simple elastic experiments, and other science topics.

EARTH SCIENCE

Atmosphere

DID YOU KNOW?

*Some weather information comes
from exploding balloons!*

The **atmosphere** is the blanket of gases called **air** that surrounds the Earth. Without several of the atmospheric gases, life on Earth could not exist. The physical processes in the atmosphere, such as movement, are responsible for the Earth's varied climates.

Aristotle promoted the idea that air was one of the four basic substances (earth, air, fire, and water), called elements, from which everything was made. He taught that each of these elements could be changed into the other, so air could turn into water, earth, or fire. In the seventeenth century, Aristotle's ideas about elements were finally challenged. One discovery by scientists was that air is a mixture of different gases, including oxygen and carbon dioxide. (See chapter 16 for more information about elements.)

Weather is the condition of the atmosphere in a specific place at a particular time. The study of weather is called **meteorology** and people who study weather are called **meteorologists.** Modern study of meteorology began with two inventions. First, the **thermometer,** an instrument used to measure **temperature** (how hot or cold something is), was invented by Galileo in 1593. In 1643, the **barometer** an instrument used to measure air pressure (also called **atmospheric pressure** or **barometric pressure**), was invented by Galileo's student Evangelista Torricelli (1608–1647), an Italian mathematician and scientist. Scientists soon discovered that weather conditions are related to temperature and pressure changes, and by the end of the seventeenth century, records of atmospheric conditions were being kept at many locations. (See chapter 18 and 25 for more on air pressure.)

Using such records, the American statesman and scientist Benjamin Franklin (1706–1790) first determined that a **storm** is a fast-moving **air mass** or large body of air that is about the same temperature, pressure, and **humidity** (water content) throughout. The Norwegian meteorologists Vilhelm Bjerknes (1862–1951) and his son Jacob (1897–1975) discovered that some air masses do not mix together due to differences in their temperature or **density** (mass per unit volume). They called the boundary between different air masses a **front.** It was not until the 1850s, when the telegraph was in use, that information about the weather from many different locations could be shared and weather forecasts made.

During the latter half of the nineteenth century, weather balloons were used to probe the upper levels of the atmosphere. Balloons are still used to study the upper atmosphere. Some balloons explode, allowing the weather instruments inside to be parachuted to Earth. The balloons burst because they are filled with a light gas such as helium. As the balloon rises, there is less pressure on it and the gas inside **expands** (becomes greater in size) due to molecules moving farther apart. Thus the balloon enlarges. Each balloon can be stretched to a certain size without breaking, but if stretched more, the balloon bursts.

Early investigations with weather balloons resulted in the discovery of a layer of the atmosphere that is different from that directly above Earth. Today the atmosphere is known to have five basic layers. Differences between the layers include their distance from Earth, the density of air, their temperature, and what happens there. (See "Fun Time!" for a model of the layers of the atmosphere.)

In the 1920s, the **radiosonde** was developed. A radiosonde is an instrument, carried by a balloon into the atmosphere, that measures temperature, pressure, and humidity and sends the information back to Earth by radio. This instrument allowed changes in the atmosphere to be monitored.

During World War II (1939–1945), pilots discovered narrow streams of high-speed winds moving from west to east in the upper part of the **troposphere** (layer of the atmosphere nearest the surface of the Earth) at altitudes of about 6 miles (9.6 km). These fast-moving winds that encircle Earth, called **jet streams,** move because Earth rotates about its axis.

The first global view of the atmosphere came from the information from *Trios I,* a man-made satellite, and the first weather satellite, which was launched in 1960. Between 1964 and 1978, seven more satellites were launched. Many more are now in orbit. Satellites send hundreds of thousands of measurements and observations to meteorologists each day. With the development of high-speed computers, this information can be easily organized and weather forecasts for any part of the world made in a short time.

FUN TIME!

Purpose

To make Earth's atmospheric layers.

Materials

pen
ruler
sheet of white copy paper

Procedure

1. Starting 2 inches (5 cm) from the top of the paper, use the pen and ruler to draw an 8-by-9-inch (20-by-22.5 cm) rectangle.

2. Starting at the top of the rectangle, use the pen and ruler to draw six dashed lines 1½ inches (3.75 cm) apart across the paper.

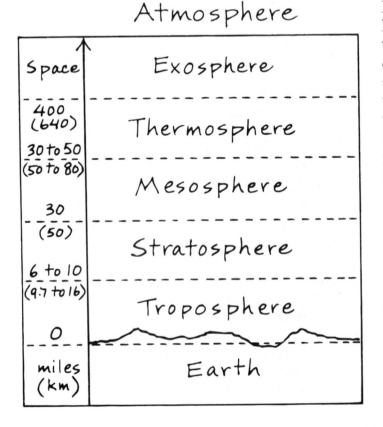

3. Draw a line from the top to the bottom and 1 inch (2.5 cm) from the left side of the rectangle.

4. Write "ATMOSPHERE" at the top of the paper and add the names of the atmospheric layers in order from top to bottom as shown: Exosphere, Ionosphere, Mesosphere, Stratosphere, Troposphere.

5. Add the altitude measurements down the left side and an arrowhead at the top.

6. Draw some land features of Earth extending above the 0-mile (0-km) altitude.

Results

You have made a model of Earth's atmosphere.

Why?

Earth's atmosphere is divided into five basic layers. Starting with the outer layer, they are the exosphere, ionosphere, mesosphere, stratosphere, and troposphere. While the model shows a specific starting point for each layer, there is no real barrier dividing each layer, and the layers vary in attitude at different points on Earth. For example, at Earth's equator the troposphere is about 32 miles (20 km) high, but at the poles it is only about 5 miles (8 km) high.

MORE FUN WITH THE ATMOSPHERE!

Air masses form when air stays over a region long enough to take on the temperature and humidity characteristics of that region. It takes a week or more for an air mass to form.

Temperature affects the density of air masses because the warm air is more expanded. Warm air masses are less dense than cold air masses, and humid air masses are less dense than dry air masses. When air masses with different densities meet, the two masses do not mix. When a warm air mass enters an area covered by a cold air mass, the warm air mass moves over the top of the cold air mass and a distinct boundary forms between the air masses.

You can model a front by mixing two **immiscible** (unmixable) liquids, such as oil and water. Do this by filling a 1-cup (250-mL) measuring cup with tap water. Add three drops of blue food coloring to the water and stir. Pour the water into a 20-ounce (600-mL) clear plastic bottle. Fill the measuring cup with oil. Tilt the bottle of water and slowly pour the oil into the bottle. Observe the movement of the oil into the bottle.

BOOK LIST

Allaby, Michael. *How the Weather Works*. Pleasantville, N.Y.: Reader's Digest Association, 1995. Outline the history of meteorology and provides weather experiments.

VanCleave, Janice. *Janice VanCleave's Weather*. New York: Wiley, 1995. Experiments about air masses and other weather topics. Each chapter contains ideas that can be turned into award-winning science fair projects.

Williams, Jack. *The Weather Book*. New York: Vintage Books, 1992. An easy-to-understand guide to weather in the United States.

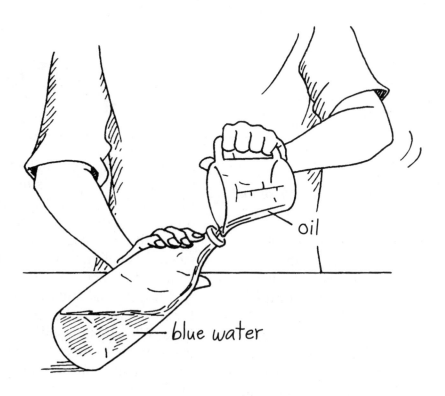

oil

blue water

Earth's Shape

DID YOU KNOW?

Disappearing ships gave clues to Earth's shape!

From about 2000 B.C., astronomers in Babylon (an ancient city near present-day Baghdad, Iraq) studied the Earth and celestial bodies. Many viewed Earth as being flat and **finite** (having limits). They assumed that if you traveled far enough, you would reach the point where Earth and sky meet. The Babylonians' view of the universe pictured Earth as having a domelike shell above it called the firmament. This dome rotated, which explained the motion of celestial bodies in the sky.

In the seventh century B.C., the Greek philosopher Thales (625–547 B.C.) described

Earth as being essentially a flat island riding on an infinite sea. His student Anaximander (610–c.547 B.C.) disagreed. Anaximander thought Earth was the shape of a short cylinder, with Greece and other lands on the upper face. This cylinder was situated in the center of an infinite space.

Both the flat and cylindrical models of Earth's shape conflicted with several known facts. When a ship sailed far enough away from shore, it not only became smaller in apparent size but eventually appeared to sink into the water, and appeared to rise from the water when it later returned to shore. If Earth were flat, then ships sailing away from shore would get smaller due to distance but would continue to be fully seen. Only a **spherical** (ball-shaped) Earth could explain the apparent disappearance of ships over the horizon. The idea of a spherical Earth is credited to the Greek mathematician Pythagoras of Samos (c.580–c.500 B.C.).

The spherical Earth model was further supported by what happens during a lunar eclipse. The Greeks knew that an eclipse of the Moon is caused by the Moon moving into the shadow of Earth. Aristotle observed that the line between light and dark on the Moon's surface during an eclipse was curved and always had the same amount of curvature. He argued that if Earth were any shape other than spherical, it would not always cast a curved shadow on the Moon.

Later the Greek mathematician Eratosthenes (c.276-c.194 B.C.) stood sticks in the ground in two different cities at the same **longitude.** Longitude is a location along an imaginary line from Earth's North Pole (most northern point) to its South Pole (most southern point). The sticks stood upright and at right angles to Earth. The shadow cast by each stick was measured at the same time of day. Eratosthenes knew that if Earth were flat, the angles of the shadows would be the same, but since Earth is spherical, the angles of the shadows were different. Using the distance between the two cities and the difference in the angles of the shadows, Eratosthenes calculated the **circumference** (distance around a circle) of the Earth. His calculations were very close to today's measurement of Earth's circumference.

Eratosthenes and other ancient Greeks scientifically proved Earth to be a sphere, but it was not until the sixteenth century, when the Portuguese navigator Ferdinand Magellan (c.1480–1521) led the first expedition to **circumnavigate** (travel completely around) the world, that it was directly shown that Earth has no "ends."

Today spacecraft orbit Earth, further confirming that Earth is spherical. But instead of being a perfect sphere, Earth is an **oblate spheroid** (a sphere that is flattened at the poles and bulging at the equator). This has been determined by comparing two measurements. One measurement is the circumference of Earth from pole to pole. The other measurement is the circumference at the equator.

FUN TIME!

Purpose

To model a ship disappearing over the horizon.

Materials

pencil

1-by-3-inch (2.5-by-7.5-cm) strip of white copy paper

20-inch (50-cm) piece of string

basketball (or any large ball)

Procedure

1. Use the pencil to draw a ship on the strip of paper.

2. Lay the string across the table so that one end of the string is in line with the table's edge.

3. Kneel next to the table at eye level with the end of the string.

4. Stand the paper with the ship facing you at the end of the string near the table's edge.

5. Move the paper to the opposite end of the string. As you move the paper, note how visible the ship is during the motion.

6. Place the ball near the edge of the table and lay the string over the top of the ball so that half of the string is on either side of the ball.

7. Kneel next to the table again at eye level with the end of the string.

8. Stand the paper at the end of the string and, without moving your head, move the paper to the opposite end of the string. Note how visible the ship is during this motion.

Results

The ship is visible when you move it along the flat table, but it moves out of view behind the ball.

Why?

Where the Earth and sky seem to meet is called the horizon. Because Earth is curved, ships appear to sink in the sea as they move away from shore and below the horizon. In this investigation, the paper ship slowly disappeared from sight as it moved over the curved surface of the ball and below the "horizon."

MORE FUN WITH EARTH'S SHAPE!

To understand the importance of Earth's curved shadow on the Moon, scientists had to know what shape would produce the shadow. They may have used differently shaped objects and studied the shape of the shadow. You can copy their investigation by taping a sheet of paper to the wall and standing a desk lamp about 2 feet (60 cm) or more from the paper. Using clay, make different shapes, including a sphere. Place each clay model one at a time on a pencil. In a darkened room, hold the clay model between the lamp and the paper. Move each clay model so that as many differently shaped shadows as possible are produced.

BOOK LIST

Filkin, David. *Stephen Hawking's Universe*. New York: Basic Books, 1997. A brief history of the cosmos and other astronomy.

Hathaway, Nancy. *The Friendly Guide to the Universe*. New York: Penguin Books, 1994. A down-to-Earth tour of space, time, and the wonders of the universe.

VanCleave, Janice. *Janice VanCleave's Earth Science for Every Kid*. New York: Wiley, 1991. Fun, simple earth science experiments, including information about the Earth's shape.

Thermometer

DID YOU KNOW?

Thermometers have been made with air, water, mercury, alcohol, crystals, and even wine!

Temperature is a measure of how hot or cold something is. Although observations about air temperature were made by early humans, **quantitative** (expresses as a quantity) measurements could not be made until the invention of the thermometer.

In 1593, Galileo designed the first crude thermometer, which he called a "thermoscope." This air thermometer was made from a bulb-shaped glass container about the size of a hen's egg with a narrow tube about 16 inches (40 cm) long. Galileo would warm the bulb by squeezing it in his hands, then insert the tube into a container of water. When the bulb cooled, the air inside contracted, and the water rose in the tube to fill the space. The thermoscope did not have a scale, so only **qualitative** (expressed as a quality or characteristic) measurements, such as hot, warm, cool, or very cool, could be made. But even without a scale, Galileo's air thermometer could be used to more accurately compare temperatures of materials than by just feeling them.

The design of Galileo's thermoscope was based on the fact that gases expand when heated and contract when cooled. In 1632, The French physician Jean Rey (1582–1645) designed a liquid thermometer. This instrument worked because, like gases, liquids expand and contract when heated. The ends of the tubes in Galileo's and Rey's thermometers were open. In 1654, Ferdinand II de' Medici (1610–1670), the Grand Duke of Tuscany, Italy, designed a sealed liquid-in-glass thermometer. It was unscaled and used wine instead of water.

Galileo's and Rey's thermometers had no fixed scale. To have a scale, there must be a standard reference point. Reference points that were suggested included the melting point of butter and the temperature of blood. Eventually a scale with two reference points, the freezing and boiling points of water, was chosen. These points are still used in modern thermometers.

Daniel Gabriel Fahrenheit (1686–1736), a German scientist, introduced the alcohol thermometer in 1709, and the mercury thermometer in 1714. He introduced a temperature scale in 1724. The Fahrenheit scale that still bears his name is still widely used in Britain and the United States (although seldom in scientific work). The Celsius scale, called the Centigrade scale until 1948, is favored by scientists. This temperature scale was named for the Swedish astronomer Anders Celsius (1701–1744). In the original scale devised by Celsius in 1742, 0° was assigned to the boiling point of water, 100° to the freezing point. This was soon reversed. Some say that Carolus Linnaeus (1707–1778), a Swedish botanist,

reversed the scale, and it is this scale that is used today.

Many types of thermometers are used today. One type of thermometer for measuring body temperature has a narrow section in the tube that stops liquid from going back into the bulb until the thermometer is shaken. This gives the user time to read the temperature. Since thermometers do get broken and mercury is toxic (poisonous), other liquids started being used in thermometers, such as alcohol and dye. But, since alcohol is flammable, a safer vegetable oil–type liquid and dye is most recently being used.

Some thermometers are flexible strips coated with special crystals. The crystals reflect different colors of light depending on the position of their molecules, which changes depending on temperature.

FUN TIME!

Purpose

To make a model of Galileo's air thermometer.

Materials

ruler
tap water
1-quart (1-L) jar
red food coloring
drinking straw
glass soda bottle
golf ball–size piece of modeling clay
timer

Procedure

1. Pour about 2 inches (5 cm) of water into the jar.

2. Add drops of food coloring to the water to make the water a deep red color.

3. Insert about 2 inches (5 cm) of one end of the straw into the mouth of the soda bottle.

4. Mold the clay around the straw to seal the mouth of the bottle.

5. Turn the bottle upside down and stand it in the jar. The jar should support the bottle with the open end of the straw just above the bottom of the jar. The straw should extend below the surface of the water. If necessary, reposition the straw in the bottle to adjust its length outside the bottle.

6. Remove the bottle and hold it in your hands. Wrap your hands around the sides of the bottle. Press as much of the palms of your hands as possible against the glass, but do not press hard enough to break the glass.

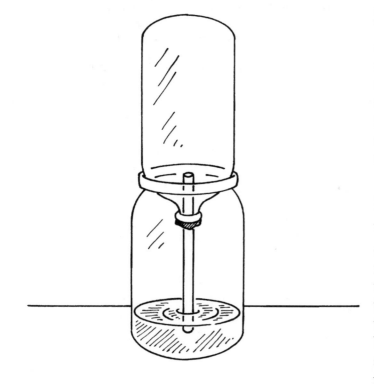

7. At the end of 1 minute, turn the bottle upside down and stand it, straw side down, in the jar of colored water as in step 5.

8. Observe the straw for 2 or more minutes.

Results

The colored water rises in the straw and flows into the bottle.

Why?

The bottle is a simple model of Galileo's thermoscope. Both make use of the fact that a gas expands when heated and contracts when cooled. The bottle and straw are filled with air. Holding the bottle in your hand causes the gas inside to be heated. The heated gas molecules move more quickly. The gas expands and the molecules move farther apart, escaping through the open end of the straw. As the bottle cools, the gas molecules move more slowly. The gas contracts and the molecules move closer together. Since there are now fewer gas molecules in the bottle, they take up less space and a partial vacuum is created. The air pressure that is inside the bottle is less than inside the jar above the water, so air pressure on the surface of the water forces the water into the straw.

MORE FUN WITH EXPANDING GAS!

Without touching a bottle, you can make a coin covering the bottle's mouth rise and fall as if by magic. Place an empty 2-L plastic soda bottle in the freezer. After 5 or more minutes, remove the bottle from the freezer. Immediately cover the mouth of the bottle with a quarter that has been dipped in water. Within seconds, the coin starts to make a clicking sound as it rises and falls.

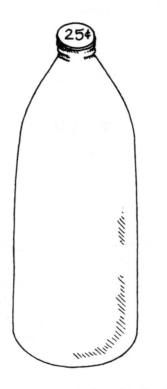

Cooling causes the air inside the bottle to contract and more air enters. When the bottle is removed from the freezer the cold air in the bottle starts to heat up and expand. The gas exerts enough pressure on the coin to cause it to rise on one side. The coin falls when some of the gas escapes. This process continues until the gas inside the bottle does not exert enough pressure to lift the coin. This occurs when the temperature inside the bottle is at or near that outside the bottle. The coin will also stop clicking if it falls into a position that leaves a space for the gas to escape through. If this happens, try rewetting and repositioning the coin.

BOOK LIST

Chaloner, Jack. *Hot and Cold.* New York: Raintree Steck-Vaughn, 1997. Simple activities that introduce the concepts of hot and cold and explore temperatures in different regions of Earth, including desert and polar areas.

Gardner, Robert, and Eric Kemer. Science *Projects about Temperature and Heat.* Springfield, N.J.: Enslow, 1994. Simple experiments about thermometers and other heat-related topics.

VanCleave, Janice. *Janice VanCleave's Weather.* New York: Wiley, 1995. Experiments about temperature and other weather topics. Each chapter contains ideas that can be turned into award-winning science fair projects.

Walpole, Brenda. *Temperature.* Milwaukee: Gareth Stevens, 1995. Facts and activities about temperature, including the history of the development of the thermometer.

Compasses

DID YOU KNOW?

Hanging stones can give directions!

A **compass** is an instrument that indicates direction on the Earth's surface. One of the most common types of compass is the magnetic compass, which contains a magnetic needle. The earth acts like a large magnet. A magnet is an object that has a strong **magnetic field,** which is a space around it that attracts magnetic materials (such as iron). The attraction that magnets have on magnetic materials is called **magnetic force** or **magnetism.** The compass needle responds to Earth's magnetic field. The ends of magnets are called the **north pole** and the **south pole.** The north pole

points to a place on Earth called the **magnetic north pole** (an area near Earth's northernmost point—**North Pole**). The south pole points to Earth's **magnetic south pole** (an area near Earth's southernmost point—South Pole). (See chapter 4 for more about magnets.)

It is not known who exactly invented the first magnetic compass, but magnetism has been known since ancient times. The Greeks, the Romans, and the Chinese used **magnetite,** a naturally magnetic mineral that is an iron ore and attracts iron objects. It is believed that the first crude compass was nothing more than a piece of magnetite suspended form a string. Early travelers called the mineral **lodestone,** meaning "leading stone."

The earliest magnetic needle compasses were made by magnetizing iron needles. This was done by rubbing them on a piece of lodestone. There are two types of magnetic compass, the dry compass and the liquid compass. In a dry compass, the magnetized needle was suspended from a string. Floating the magnetized needle on a chip of wood in a bowl of water produced a wet compass. The needles in both dry and wet compasses always point in a north—south direction. The wet compass was more useful at sea because the needle remained steady even when the compass was bounced around by waves. It was not until the 1200s that European seamen first used a magnetic compass at sea.

In the past, ships were made mostly of wood, but today they are made of steel, an iron alloy. A magnetic compass mounted on a steel ship is put in a special container so that it won't be influenced by the ship's magnetism. In aircraft, the magnetic compass is often located at a position outside the plane, where the magnetism of the craft has the least effect. From this location, compass directions are transmitted electronically to the cockpit. This kind of compass is called a transmitting compass.

FUN TIME!

Purpose

To make a wet compass.

Materials

drawing compass
Styrofoam plate
scissors
small paper clip
strong magnet
bowl

tap water
directional compass
marking pen

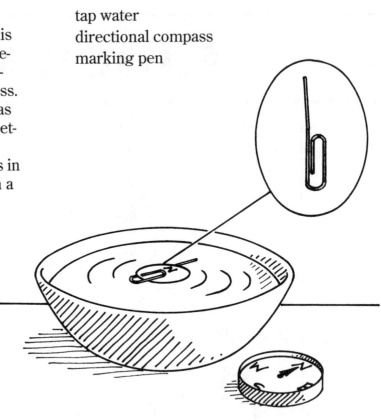

Procedure

1. Use the drawing compass to draw a 1-inch (2.5-cm) circle on the bottom of the Styrofoam plate. Cut out the circle and discard the rest of the plate.

2. Bend one end of the paper clip straight.

3. Magnetize the paper clip by laying it on the magnet for 1 or more minutes.

4. Clip the paper clip to the Styrofoam circle.

5. Fill the bowl with water and set the Styrofoam circle in the water.

6. When the circle stops moving, use the directional compass to determine which end of the paper clip points north.

7. Remove the circle from the water and write "N" on the end of the circle that points north.

8. Return the circle to the bowl and slowly rotate the bowl. Observe the direction the floating paper clip points.

Results

One end of the floating paper clip points north. When the bowl is turned, the paper clip continues to point in the same direction.

Why?

In a wet compass, the magnetized needle floats in a bowl filled with a liquid. This produces the minimum possible friction, allowing the needle to rotate easily. When the bowl, like a ship, turns, the magnetized needle continues to point north.

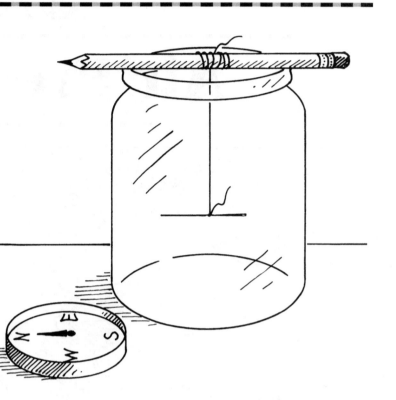

MORE FUN WITH COMPASSES!

In a dry compass, friction can be reduced by suspending the magnetized needle from a thread. To make a dry compass, magnetize a long sewing needle by laying it on a magnet for 1 or more minutes. Tie one end of a 12-inch (30-cm) piece of sewing thread around the needle. Move the needle in the loop of thread until it balances when suspended from the thread. Tie the free end of the thread around the center of a pencil. Then lower the needle into a 1-quart (1-L) jar so that the needle hangs approximately in the center of the jar. Wind the thread around the pencil and lay the pencil across the mouth of the jar. Use the compass to determine which end of the needle points north.

BOOK LIST

VanCleave, Janice. *Janice VanCleave's Magnets*. New York: Wiley, 1993. Experiments about compasses and other magnet topics. Each chapter contains ideas that can be turned into award-winning science fair projects.

Waters, Kate. *Compass*. New York: Scholastic, 1996. Explains how people from different cultures at different time periods used compasses. Includes a kit with materials to make compasses

Wiese, Jim. *Rocket Science*. New York: Wiley, 1995. Fifty science gadgets kids can create themselves, including a compass.

25

Air Pressure

DID YOU KNOW?

Caves can indicate air pressure!

The air in Earth's atmosphere is made up of billions of molecules moving around in every direction and constantly bumping into everything around them. These collisions result in what is known as air pressure. The density of air affects the number of collisions and therefore the air pressure. As the density of air increases, the number of molecules in a specific volume of air increases, thus collisions increase and so does air pressure. As the density of air decreases, the reverse is true.

Long before instruments were designed to measure air pressure, nature indicated pressure changes. One of the more dramatic natural indicators of an approaching storm was air rushing out of caves. Before a storm, air pressure decreases. The air pressure outside the cave is less than the air pressure inside. Air moves from higher to lower pressure, so the air would rush out of the cave opening.

In 1643 an instrument called a barometer was invented to measure air pressure. Galileo had investigated the behavior of water in long tubes, but it was his student Evangelista Torricelli who invented the first barometer, called a **mercury barometer.** Torricelli determined that it was changes in air pressure that made liquid in the tubes rise and fall. Galileo's water tubes were about 36 feet (11 m) long.

Torricelli created his own tubes, which were only about 2 feet (0.6 m) long and he used mercury instead of water. Since mercury's density is 13 times that of water, it only takes one-thirteenth as much mercury as water for the two substances to have the same mass. The mercury-filled tube was sealed on one end and the tube was inverted with its open end in a bowl of mercury. Torricelli correctly hypothesized that the pressure of the air pushing on the surface of the mercury in the bowl would push the mercury up the tube. He observed that the height of the mercury changed from day to day, indicating that the air pressure changed as well.

Torricelli died before he could further investigate and prove his hypothesis. This proof was provided by the investigations of a French scientist, Blaise Pascal (1623–1662). Pascal designed an experiment and sent helpers to perform it. His investigation was to set different mercury barometers along a mountain slope. If Torricelli was correct, there would be less air pressure at the top of the mountain and the mercury in the tube would drop as greater heights were reached. This was exactly what the experiment showed.

There have been many improvements on Torricelli's mercury barometer, but the basic design—a tube of mercury in an exposed container of mercury—is the same. Another type of barometer, called the **aneroid barometer,** uses a thin, stretched material to register changes in air pressure.

FUN TIME!

Purpose

To demonstrate air pressure.

Materials

push pin
small plastic soda bottle
tap water
6-inch (15-cm) round balloon
adult helper

Procedure

1. Use the pushpin to poke a hole in the side of the bottle near the bottom. If this is difficult, ask an adult to help.

2. Set the bottle in a sink and fill it by holding it under the faucet.

3. Set the bottle on the counter with the hole pointing toward the sink. Observe the flow of water out the hole in the bottle.

4. After a few seconds, stretch the mouth of the balloon over the mouth of the bottle. Again observe the hole in the bottle.

Results

Water streams out the hole in the bottle when the bottle's mouth is open. When the bottle's mouth is closed by the balloon, water continues

balloon inside the bottle

to come out of the hole for a short time, then it stops. As the water streams out of the bottle, part of the balloon moves into the mouth of the bottle.

WHY?

When the mouth of the bottle is open, air is pressing down on the surface of the water in the bottle. Air is also pressing against the water through the hole in the side of the bottle. Air pressure on the water's surface plus the weight of the water creates a pressure greater than the air pressure outside the small hole in the bottle, so water streams out the hole. When the mouth of the bottle is closed, water continues to stream out the hole for a time reducing its height and allowing the air inside the bottle to expand, thus reducing its density. As the depth of the water and density of the air decrease their pressure decreases. With less pressure inside the bottle, the greater air pressure outside pushes part of the balloon into the bottle, thus compressing the air inside the bottle and increasing its density and pressure. When the pressure inside the bottle and air pressure on the hole outside the bottle are equal, the water stops flowing.

MORE FUN WITH AIR PRESSURE!

Air pressure was used to help push the water out of the bottle. Air pressure can also be used to keep water from entering a container. Demonstrate this by filling a bucket half full with water. Crumple a large paper napkin or paper towel into a ball and push it in to the bottom of a 10-ounce (300-mL) clear plastic glass. Turn the glass upside down. The paper wad must remain against the bottom of the glass. (Make the paper ball a little bigger if it falls out.) Holding the glass with its mouth pointing down, push the glass straight down into the bucket of water. Do not tilt the glass as you lift it out of the water. Remove the paper and examine it. It will be dry because the air in the glass prevented the water from entering the glass.

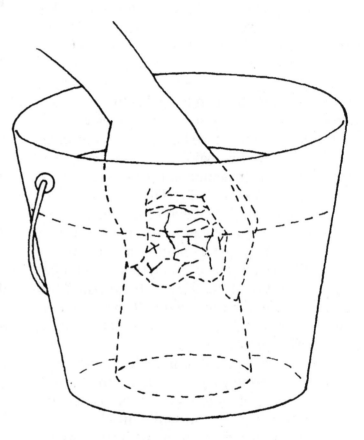

BOOK LIST

Lockhart, Gary. *The Weather Companion.* New York: Wiley, 1988. History, science, legend, and folklore about air pressure and other weather topics.

Spencer, Christian. *Can It Really Rain Frogs?* New York: Wiley, 1997. Facts and fun experiments about the weather and weather instruments, including the barometer.

VanCleave, Janice. *Janice VanCleave's Weather.* New York: Wiley, 1995. Experiments about barometers and other weather topics. Each chapter contains ideas that can be turned into award-winning science fair projects.

VI

PHYSICS

Rubber

DID YOU KNOW?

Rubber got its name because it could rub out pencil marks!

Natural rubber is an **elastic** (able to return to the original shape after being stretched), water-repellent substance found in plant **latex,** which is a milky liquid in specialized cells of some plants, particularly the tree *Hevea brasilensis,* commonly called the rubber tree. There is no record of the original discover of latex, but the Spanish navigator Christopher Columbus

(1451–1506) is given credit for being the first European to discover rubber and bring it to Europe. On his second voyage, he saw latex used to make balls that children played with as well as to waterproof materials.

For several centuries, the bouncy material was only a museum oddity in Europe. However, in time there was a scientific interest in the properties of the material. In the late eighteenth century, the English scientist Joseph Priestley (1733–1804) discovered that the bouncy material would rub out lead pencil marks, so he named it "**rubber.**" Soon after, an

English manufacturer discovered a way to waterproof cloth by treating it with a mixture of rubber and turpentine. This was the first commercial use of rubber.

Since natural rubber is very sticky when warm, the Scottish chemist and inventor Charles Macintosh (1766–1843) used warmed rubber to glue two pieces of cloth together. From this cloth he made waterproof raincoats (patented in 1823). The name "mackintosh" is still sometimes used for raincoats and the waterproof fabric they are made from.

Macintosh's waterproof material, as well as other products made with natural rubber, became a sticky goo in the summer heat and brittle in the cold temperatures of winter. Between 1830 and 1839, an American inventor, Charles Goodyear (1800–1860), worked on ways to make rubber more useful in a wide range of temperatures. After many unsuccessful attempts to change rubber, he accidentally dropped a mixture of rubber and sulfur on a hot stove. Instead of melting, the mixture charred. He called this process **vulcanization.** Goodyear didn't know why his vulcanization process worked, but he had made vulcanized rubber one of the most important and versatile products of the modern world. Vulcanized rubber has greater strength, elasticity, and durability than natural rubber. In 1898, many years after his death, the Goodyear Tire and Rubber Company was founded and named after Charles Goodyear.

The unusual chemical structure of rubber was described in 1920 by the German chemist Hermann Staudinger (1881–1965). He called the rubber molecule a polymer. **Polymers** are substances consisting of large molecules that are made up of many small, repeating units called **monomers,** or **mers.** *Polymer* comes from two Greek words, *poly* meaning "many" and *meros* meaning "parts." Once the composition of rubber was identified, **synthetic**

rubber could be explored. In the 1950s, synthetic rubber was first made from petroleum. Synthetic rubber is almost indistinguishable from natural rubber.

Today the term rubber is applied to a class of materials having the unique property of high elasticity (ability to return to the same shape after being stretched).

The flexibility of natural rubber is due to its long molecular structure. Vulcanization ties the molecules together with crosslinks like rungs on a ladder. It is the wide spacing between the crosslinks in rubber that gives it is extraordinary elasticity.

FUN TIME!

Purpose

To test the elasticity of a rubber band.

Materials

scissors
rubber band
yardstick (meterstick)
masking tape

Procedure

1. Cut the rubber band so that it is one long piece.

2. Place one end of the rubber strip over the end of the measuring stick, with about 1 inch (2.5 cm) wrapped around to the under side. Tape the rubber strip to the measuring stick by wrapping tape around the end of the stick.

3. Lay the measuring stick on a table.

4. Straighten the rubber strip without stretching it. Note the length of the rubber strip.

5. Pressing the taped end of the measuring stick with one hand, stretch the rubber strip 6 inches (15 cm).

6. While holding the taped end of the rubber strip, move the free end of the strip back to an unstretched position. *CAUTION: Do not release the strip because it may hit your other hand.* Straighten the strip and note its length.

7. Repeat steps 4 to 6, stretching the rubber strip 12 inches (30 cm) in step 5.

Results

When stretched a short distance, the rubber strip returns to its original length. When stretched a longer distance, its unstretched length may slightly increase.

Why?

The rubber band has an **elastic limit,** which is the most a material can be stretched and still return to its original size and shape without permanent **deformation** (change in shape). While the exact elastic limit was not determined, for the rubber band used, its elastic limit would be 6 to 12 inches (15 to 30 cm) . If your rubber band did not deform, you might try stretching it 4 to 6 inches (10 to 15 cm) more.

MORE FUN WITH ELASTICITY!

Rubber balloons are often difficult to inflate. But if you stretch the balloon with your hands several times before inflating it, this action deforms the rubber and makes the balloon easier to inflate. Demonstrate this using two balloons of the same size and shape. First try to inflate one of the balloons without first stretching it. Stretch the second balloon several times, then try to inflate it.

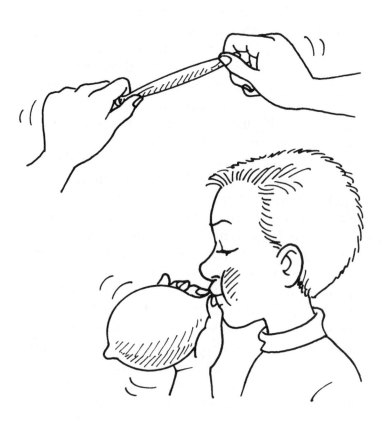

BOOK LIST

Brown, Robert J. *333 Science Tricks and Experiments.* Fort Worth, Tex.: Tandy Corporation, 1984. Science investigations including elasticity.

Haven, Kendall. *Marvels of Science.* Englewood, Colo.: Librarians Unlimited, 1994. Information about 50 marvels of science, including rubber.

VanCleave, Janice. *Janice VanCleave's 202 Oozing, Bubbling, Dripping, and Bouncing Experiments.* New York: Wiley, 1996. Fun, simple elastic experiments and other science topics.

27

Buoyancy

DID YOU KNOW?

A bathing scientist discovered buoyancy!

Before the Greek mathematician and inventor Archimedes (c.287–212 B.C.), nobody knew why some things float and others don't. It is said that Archimedes' king gave a silversmith a certain amount of gold to make him a new crown. When the crown was finished, the king asked Archimedes to figure out a way to secretly determine if the crown was made of pure gold or a mix of gold and cheaper metals, as the king suspected. Archimedes was puzzled as to how to do this, until he stepped into a bathtub and observed that his body **displaced**

(pushed out of place) a certain **volume** (amount of space that a material occupies) of water from the tub.

Gold has a specific density, or mass per unit volume. This means that there is a specific amount of gold material in a given volume. Archimedes realized that he could determine the volume of the crown by measuring the volume of water displaced by the crown, and using the volume and the mass of the crown, he could determine it density. It is said that he was so excited about his discovery that he ran naked through the street yelling, "Eureka!" (I have found it!). He determined that the density of the crown was not that of pure gold, and the silversmith who made the crown was killed for stealing from the king.

Whether this story is true or not, Archimedes did discover a technique for determining density using water displacement. He also discovered that fluids, such as air or water, apply an upward **buoyant force** on objects less dense than themselves that are partially or totally submerged in the fluids. Such objects are said to have **buoyancy.** The buoyant force is equal to the weight of the fluid that the object displaces. This natural law is called **Archimedes' principle.**

Whether a material floats or sinks in a fluid doesn't depend on its weight but rather on its density. An object with a density greater than that of the fluid it is in sinks, while an object with a lesser density floats. This explains why a heavy ship can float. Because the ship is hollow, the weight is spread out and the ship displaces a large volume of water. According to Archimedes' principle, the weight of this displaced water is equal to the buoyant force pushing up on the ship. If the ship were **compressed** (pressed together) into a solid block, it would weigh the same but its density would be greater than water and it would sink. The small solid block would displace less water than the large hollow ship and its buoyancy (tendency to float) would be less.

FUN TIME!

Purpose

To determine how a heavy ship floats.

Materials

two 12-inch (30-cm) –squares pieces of aluminum foil
20 paper clips
small bucket
tap water

Procedure

1. Wrap one of the foil squares around 10 paper clips and squeeze the foil into a tight ball.

2. Fold up the four edges of the second foil square to make a small boat. Place the remaining 10 paper clips in the boat. Spread the clips as evenly as possible.

3. Fill the bucket with water.

4. Set the foil boat and ball on the surface of the water in the bucket and observe what happens.

Results

The boat floats and the ball sinks.

Why?

The ball and the boat both have the same weight, but the ball has a smaller volume than the boat. The weight of water displaced by an object equals the buoyant force of water pushing upward on the object. Because the boat is hollow it has a larger volume, thus it displaces more water than does the solid ball, therefore there is more buoyant force on the boat, enough to cause it to float. Ships are very heavy, but they have a large volume, which increases their buoyancy.

MORE FUN WITH BUOYANCY!

Fish rise and sink in water by changing their density. They can do this by increasing or decreasing the volume of air inside a special balloonlike body part called a **swim bladder.** You can demonstrate this by placing a condiment packet inside a bottle of water. First decide which condiment packet will make the best model fish. Do this by filling a jar about three-fourths full with tap water and dropping different packets into the water. The best model fish is the packet that is just barely submerged below the water's surface.

Insert the condiment packet in a 2-L plastic soda bottle. Fill the bottle to overflowing with tap water. Secure the cap on the bottle, then squeeze the bottle with your hands. The pressure of the water on the packet causes the air in the packet to be compressed, so the air bubble shrinks. When the air bubble in the packet

is smaller, the packet's volume decreases and its density increases. The greater density causes the packet to sink. When you release the pressure on the bottle, air is decompressed and the air bubble expands. The density of the packet decreases which makes the packet rise.

BOOK LIST

Haven, Kendall. *Marvels of Science.* Englewood, Colo.: Librarians Unlimited, 1994. Information about 50 marvels of science, including Archimedes' discovery of buoyancy.

Meikle, Marg. *Funny You Should Ask.* New York: Scholastic, 1999. Weird but true answers to more than 100 questions, including questions about buoyancy.

Nye, Bill. *Bill Nye the Science Guy's Consider the Following.* New York: Scholastic, 1995. Science questions and answers, including questions about buoyancy.

VanCleave, Janice. *Janice VanCleave's 202 Oozing, Bubbling, Dripping, and Bouncing Experiments.* New York: Wiley, 1996. Fun, simple elastic experiments and other science topics.

28

Magnets

DID YOU KNOW?

Some stones have invisible forces around them!

A magnet is an object that can attract a magnetic material. Magnetic materials include those containing iron, cobalt, and nickel, the most common being iron. The attraction that magnets have for magnetic materials is called magnetic force or magnetism. The space around a magnetic material where a magnetic force can be detected is called a magnetic field.

No one knows when magnetism was first discovered, but there is evidence that ancient Chinese, Romans, and Greeks knew about it. It is believed that the Greeks found stones in an ancient place called Magnesia (in the northeastern part of the Greek peninsula) that could attract pieces of iron. The stones were first called "Magnete stones" after the Magnetes a Greek people who lived in Magnesia. Later sailors used the stones to make compasses and called them lodestones, meaning "leading stones." (See chapter 24 for more on compasses.) Today the stones are known to be an iron ore and natural magnet called magnetite.

In 1300, Petrus Perigrinus de Marcourt (13th c.), a French scientist, discovered that spherical lodestones had two regions of strongest force. He discovered that these regions, which were called **poles,** were different and that some poles **repelled** (pushed away from) and others were **attracted** (drawn near) each other. These regions are now called the magnetic north and south poles. Like poles (north and north, or south and south) repel each other, and unlike poles (north and south) attract each other. In 1600 the English physician and scientist William Gilbert (1544–1603) confirmed these discoveries and concluded, correctly, that the Earth itself is a magnet, which explains why the needle of a magnetic compass is attracted to the magnetic north pole of Earth.

In the late 1700s, Charles Augustin de Coulomb (1736–1806), a French physicist, concluded that regardless of how small the pieces into which a magnet might be subdivided, each piece would always retain a north and a south pole. In 1820, Hans Christian Oersted (1777–1851), a Danish physicist, discovered a direct relationship between electricity and magnetism by showing that an **electric current** (flow of charges) flowing in a wire caused a nearby compass needle to move. This discovery led to the invention in 1825 of the **electromagnet** (a magnet produced by an electric current) by William Sturgeon (1783–1850), an English electrical engineer.

A typical electromagnet consists of an iron core surrounded by a coil of wire carrying a direct electric current. The iron core is magnetized by the electricity. The magnetic effect of electromagnets can be controlled by changing the current through the wire. Electromagnets are found in televisions and some loudspeakers.

During the 1830s, the English scientist Michael Faraday (1791–1867) introduced the idea of **magnetic lines of force** (a pattern of lines representing the magnetic field around a magnet). These invisible lines extend through the space surrounding the magnet, running from the magnetic north pole to the magnetic south pole.

FUN TIME!

Purpose

To produce a pattern that shows the lines of force around a disk magnet.

Materials

scissors
12-inch (30-cm) pipe cleaner
disk magnet

Procedure

1. Cut the pipe cleaner into twelve 1-inch (2.5-cm) pieces.

2. Lay the magnet on a nonmetallic table.

3. Hold one of the pipe cleaner pieces upright about ½ inch (1.25 cm) above the magnet, then drop it straight down onto the magnet. Drop all the pieces this way, one at a time.

4. Observe the pattern the pipe cleaner pieces make around the magnet.

Results

The pipe cleaner pieces on the outside of the magnet lean outward at an angle, while those in the center stand more vertically.

Why?

A magnetic field is the area of force around a magnet, in which the magnet affects the movement of magnetic materials. The pipe cleaner pieces contain a thin steel (iron alloy) wire, which is pulled toward the magnet when the wire enters the magnet's magnetic field. The arrangement of the pipe cleaner pieces indicates the direction of the lines of force in the magnet's magnetic field.

MORE FUN WITH MAGNETS!

The magnetic field of a magnet can move through some materials, such as paper, as if they were not there. Demonstrate this by making a racing game. Draw a racetrack on a piece of corrugated cardboard. Support the track with legs made from empty paper towel tubes. Draw two racing cars on poster board, then cut out and color the cars. Tape a small metal paper clip to the underside of each car. Tape a small magnet to the end of each two dowels. Race the cars with a friend by holding the dowels under the racetrack so that their magnets are beneath the magnets on the cars.

BOOK LIST

Parker, Steve. *Magnets*. New York: Lorenz Books, 1997. Information about different kinds of magnets and how they are used, as well as experiments using magnets.

VanCleave, Janice. *Janice VanCleave's Magnets*. New York: Wiley, 1993. Experiments about electromagnets, magnetic lines of forces, and other magnet topics. Each chapter contains ideas that can be turned into award-winning science fair projects.

Vecchione, Glen. *Magnet Science*. New York: Sterling, 1995. Information about magnets, including what gives them power to attract or repel each other.

29

Energy

DID YOU KNOW?

A teenager made an interesting discovery about energy!

Physics is the study of matter and energy. Matter is materials and energy the mover of materials. Understanding matter is easier than understanding energy. Matter is stuff; it has weight and takes up space; it can be seen, felt, smelled, and touched. Energy is not tangible (touchable). It was from thinking about why objects move that scientists first began to develop the idea of energy.

The Greek philosopher Aristotle thought that an object moving through the air compressed the air it moved through, causing the compressed air to rush around to the rear of the object and push the object forward. But in 1583, at the age of 19, the Italian scientist Galileo observed that a swinging church lamp swung upward very nearly as high as the point from which it had previously swung downward. He used his pulse to time the swinging lamp and discovered that the time of the upswing was equal to that of the downswing. Galileo couldn't explain why the lamp swung back and forth, but he knew air rushing behind it wasn't the explanation.

Galileo's observation laid the groundwork for future scientists who further experimented and explained the types of energy involved in the movement of the swinging lamp. Gottfried Wilhelm Leibniz (1646–1716), a German mathematician devised a formula to measure the energy of motion he called "vis viva," or living force, which is now called **kinetic energy** (energy that a moving object has because of its motion). In 1803, L. N. M. Carnot (1753–1823), a French military strategist, identified what he called "latent vis viva," which is now know as **potential energy** (energy of position or condition of an object that can be changed into kinetic energy). In 1807, Thomas Young, an English physicist (1773–1829), was the first to use the word *energy* to describe the phenomenon called vis viva. He also defined energy as the ability to do work. **Work** is the transfer of energy that occurs when a force causes an object to move.

The first form of energy as defined by Young was mechanical energy, or simply the energy of moving objects or objects capable of moving. Today, physicists generally think of energy as having two forms: kinetic energy and potential energy. So, mechanical kinetic energy is energy due to motion, and mechanical potential energy is due to its position, such as a stretched rubber band or water behind a dam.

The term "kinetic energy" comes from the Greek word *kinema,* for "motion" (which also inspired the modern term "cinema"). When a car rolls down a hill, it has kinetic energy. At the top of the hill, the car has mechanical potential energy stored up in it because of its position on the hill. This stored mechanical energy is also called **gravitational potential energy** (potential energy due to the height of an object above a surface). While all kinetic energy involves motion, potential energy describes any kind of stored energy, such as

chemical potential energy (energy tied up in chemical molecules) and gravitational potential energy.

FUN TIME!

Purpose

To identify the mechanical potential energy and mechanical kinetic energy of a pendulum.

Materials

1 cup (250 mL) dry, uncooked rice
sock
8-foot (2.4-m) string
masking tape

Procedure

1. Pour the rice in the sock and tie a knot in the sock.

2. Tie one end of the string around the knot in the sock.

3. Tape the free end of the string to the top of a doorway so that the sock hangs about 1 inch (2.5 cm) above the floor.

4. Pull the sock to one side, then release it.

5. Compare the height of the sock at points A, B, and C shown in the figure.

Results

The sock is lowest at point B. The height is about the same at points A and C for each swing, but the height decreases for both with each swing.

Why?

The swinging sock is a model of a **pendulum,** which is a suspended object that is free to swing back and forth. When a pendulum swings back and forth, energy is continually changed from mechanical potential energy to mechanical kinetic energy. The change of energy from one form to another is called **energy conversion.** When an object such as a pendulum falls, energy is converted from potential to kinetic energy. Like any pendulum, as the sock swings back and forth, energy is continually being converted. At points A and C of each swing, the pendulum stops and reverses direction. At those points, the pendulum has only potential energy and no kinetic energy. As the pendulum swings down, the potential energy continuously changes to kinetic energy so that at point B at the bottom of the swing, it has only kinetic energy and no potential energy. As the pendulum rises, the kinetic energy continuously changes to potential energy, and so on.

MORE FUN WITH PENDULUMS!

Use the hanging sock to play a type of bowling game. Remove the measuring stick and place

five or more empty, plastic soda bottles about 10 inches (25 cm) beyond one side of the doorway. Pull the sock to the opposite side and release it so that it will hit the bottles. You get two tries to knock down all the bottles. To increase the difficulty of the game, fill the bottles about one-fourth full with water and seal them with lids.

BOOK LIST

Churchill, E. Richard. *365 More Simple Science Experiments with Everyday Materials.* New York: Black Dog & Leventhal, 1998. Easy investigations, including pendulum experiments.

Suplee, Curt. *Everyday Science Explained.* Washington, D.C.: National Geographic Society, 1998. Science information that encourages readers to explore everyday life, including facts about energy conversion.

VanCleave, Janice. *Janice VanCleave's Physics for Every Kid.* New York: Wiley, 1991. Fun, simple physics experiments, including information about pendulums.

Flight

DID YOU KNOW?

An artist designed wings for humans!

Flight is the ability to move with direction through the air. Bats and most birds and insects can naturally fly by flapping their wings. Some animals, such as so-called flying fish and flying squirrels, do not fly, but instead **glide** (to move smoothly and effortlessly) through the air for short periods of time.

Through the years, humans have tried to copy the flight of birds. The Italian artist and scientist Leonardo da Vinci (1452–1519) believed in human-powered flight. Among his many scientific writings are his ideas and drawings for **ornithopters** (wing-flapping aircraft). Among his designs were strap-on wings. Other scientists before and after Leonardo had

their own ideas about ornithopters. Many built elaborate wings using feathers from birds. Not being able to lift off from the ground, these would-be flyers jumped from high places and in vain flapped their feather-covered arms as they plunged to the ground. Some were killed in their efforts to investigate the use of wings to fly. Some of the problems of the ornithopters were their design and weight, plus the fact that human muscles are not strong enough to flap the wings fast enough for flight.

The forerunner of successful flight for humans was the kite. The Chinese flew kites more than 2,000 years ago. Over the centuries, kites have been used as toys, to lift people above battlefields on military observations, and to collect weather information. But kites have been most useful in the advancement of

aviation, which is the development, operation, and use of aircraft.

In the thirteenth century, the English scientist Roger Bacon (c.1220–1292) conducted buoyancy studies that led him to the conclusion that air could support a craft in the same manner that water supports boats. In the late eighteenth century, the first lighter-than-air craft was developed by the Montgolfier brothers, Joseph Michel (1740–1810) and Jacques-Etienne (1745–1799), who were French papermakers by trade. They discovered that smoke from a fire directed into a bag made the bag buoyant. In 1782 they designed and flew their first unmanned hot-air balloon, which stayed aloft for 10 minutes. In 1783 they demonstrated their flying balloon for Louis XVI and Marie Antoinette by sending aloft and safely recovering a balloon with a sheep, a duck, and a rooster aboard.

Flights with humans were made in a Montgolfier balloon two months later. The flight lasted only 20 minutes, but it was the start of another challenge for man to fly higher, farther, and faster, and of course to be the first to circumnavigate Earth nonstop in a hot-air balloon. This honor goes to Bertrand Piccard (b.1958) of Switzerland and his partner, Brian Jones (b.1948) of England. On March 21, 1999, these airmen crossed the finish line of longitude 9.27° over Mauritania, North Africa, becoming the first balloonists to circumnavigate the globe with a nonstop, nonrefueled flight, having traveled 26,756 miles (42,810 km).

At the same time that the Montgolfiers were experimenting with hot-air balloons, French physicist J. A. C. Charles (1746–1823) developed and demonstrated a hydrogen-inflated balloon. Hydrogen soon replaced hot air as the buoyant gas for airships because hydrogen gas was so much lighter than air. An **airship** is a lighter-than-air craft equipped with a bag con-

taining a gas to lift the ship, a means of **propulsion** (a way of moving an object), means for adjusting buoyancy, and one or more **gondolas** (basketlike passenger compartment suspended below an airship) for the crew and passengers. The German-built *Hindenburg* was one of the largest airships ever built, measuring 804 feet (245 m) long. This craft, filled with hydrogen, ignited and burned on May 6, 1937, as it tried to land in Lakehurst, New Jersey. Thirty-six people were killed. Airships are still used but are filled with helium gas, which is heavier than hydrogen but lighter than air. The best property of helium is that it is nonflammable.

One of the first heavier-than-air crafts was designed by Otto Lilienthal (1848–1896), a German inventor. Lilienthal studied the flight of birds and kite designs to build and fly the first **hang glider** (a kitelike flying craft) that was capable of carrying a person. Lilienthal designed and tested a series of 18 manned gliders and, in 1891, made the first of more than 2,000 glider flights. He died when of one of his gliders crashed.

The birth of practical heavier-than-air aviation came on December 17, 1903, when Orville Wright achieved the first successful flight ever made in a self-propelled heavier-than-air craft. The Wright brothers, Wilbur (1867–1912) and Orville (1871–1948) first designed and built kites, which they sold to classmates. They continued to test kites but expanded to gliders, making more than 700 successful glider flights. The next step was to add an engine to their glider, so they designed and built a tiny engine that was connected to a pair of propellers by a bicycle chain. This engine transformed the glider into a self-powered airplane, which they originally named *Flyer I* and was commonly called Kitty Hawk.

Flyer I made only four flights for a total of 98 seconds. The first was only 12 seconds and covered a distance of 170 feet (51 m), which is shorter than the passenger area of some modern aircraft. The Wright brothers worked on perfecting the design. Their *Flyer III* was the first practical airplane, which could turn, circle, fly figure eights, and stay airborne for more than 30 minutes. The first nonstop flight around the world was made by U.S. Air Force flyers in 1949 in a plane called *Lucky Lady II*. The plane was fueled in the air and traveled at an average speed of 249 miles (398 km) per hour. The flight took 94 hours and 1 minute. Today, aircraft fly around Earth in relatively short periods of time. Some airliners are **supersonic** (faster than the speed of sound), which is about 760 miles (1220 km) per hour.

The Dutch-born Swiss scientist Daniel Bernoulli (1700–1782) discovered the basic principles of fluids, now called the **Bernoulli principle.** This principal describes the behavior of moving fluids, including air. As the speed of the fluid moving over a surface increases, the pressure of the fluid on the surface decreases. Aircraft are therefore designed so that air flows faster over the top of the wings and slower below, thus giving the craft an upward force called **lift.**

FUN TIME!

Purpose

To demonstrate lift.

Materials

thread spool
index card
pencil
scissors
pushpin

Procedure

1. Stand the spool on the index card and use the pencil to trace around the spool on the card.

2. Cut out the circle beyond the pencil outline to make a paper circle that is slightly larger around than the spool.

3. Stick the pushpin through the center of the paper circle.

4. Place the paper circle over the end of the spool so that the pin is inside the center hole of the spool.

5. Turn the spool upside down, holding the paper circle against the spool. *NOTE: The surface of the spool touching the paper must be smooth and flat.*

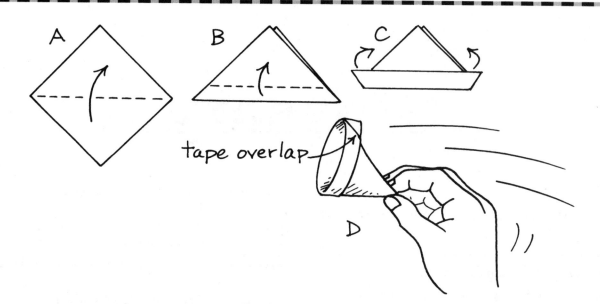

tape overlap

6. Bend over and blow through the top end of the spool as hard as possible. As you blow, stop holding the paper circle. Observe what happens to the paper circle.

7. Stop blowing and again observe what happens to the paper circle.

Results

As you blow, the paper circle sticks to the bottom of the spool. When you stop blowing, the paper circle falls.

Why?

The airstream going through the spool escapes between the spool and the paper. As the air increases in speed, it exerts less pressure on the material that it flows across. This is known as the Bernoulli principle. The air moving across the paper produces a low-pressure area between the paper and the spool as compared to the normal air pressure on the outside of the paper. The high pressure of the still air pushes the paper circle toward the spool with enough force to overcome the downward pull of gravity. The difference in pressure gives the paper circle lift.

The shape of airplane wings is such that air flows faster over the top than underneath. This difference creates enough lift on the wing to raise the plane.

MORE FUN WITH FLIGHT!

Paper airplanes are usually flat designs, but a round paper ring will also fly. Make a flying paper ring with a tail using an 8-inch (20-cm)–square piece of paper. Fold the paper as shown in steps A to C in the figure. Overlap the ends and tape them as in step D.

Fly the paper craft by placing your index and middle fingers on top of the paper tail and your thumb on the bottom as shown in step D. Raise your arm and throw the craft forward. It will not fly if thrown too hard or at the wrong angle. So practice throwing the craft in different ways to discover the best way to make it fly.

BOOK LIST

Haslam, Andrew. *Make It Work! Flight.* New York: Scholastic, 1995. Facts and fun activities about flight.

Lopex, Donald. *Flight.* Time-Life Books, 1995. Flight facts from antiquity to modern times.

VanCleave, Janice. *Janice VanCleave's Physics for Every Kid.* New York: Wiley, 1991. Fun, simple flight and other related physics investigations.

Glossary

absorb To take in.

acceleration A change or increase in the speed of an object.

agricultural Concerning farming.

air Gases in Earth's atmosphere.

air mass A large body of air that is about the same temperature, pressure, and humidity throughout.

air pressure A force that air exerts on a given area; also called **atmospheric pressure** or **barometric pressure**.

airship A lighter-than-air craft equipped with a bag containing a gas to lift the ship, a means of propulsion, means for adjusting buoyancy, and one or more gondolas for the crew and passengers.

alchemists People who practiced alchemy.

alchemy A mixture of science and magic that dealt with changing less expensive metals into gold and finding ways to prolong life indefinitely.

alloy A mixture of two or more metals or of one or more metals and a nonmetal, particularly carbon.

anatomist A scientist who studies anatomy.

anatomy The study of the structure of organisms.

aneroid barometer A type of barometer that uses a thin, stretched material to register changes in air pressure.

annealing Slow heating of metals, which makes them soft and malleable.

aphelion The farthest point from the Sun in a planet's orbit.

Archimedes' principle A natural law that states that an object in a fluid is acted upon by an upward force equal to the weight of the fluid displaced by the object.

arteries Blood vessels that carry oxygen-rich blood away from the heart.

arterioles Small blood vessels that connect capillaries with arteries.

artificial satellites Man-made bodies boosted into orbits, such as around Earth.

asteroids Small irregular bodies also called minor planets.

astronomy The study of celestial bodies.

atmosphere The blanket of air surrounding Earth.

atmospheric pressure See air pressure.

atoms Particles that scientists of the past believed were indivisible and that modern scientists have identified as the smallest building blocks of matter.

attract To cause to be drawn near.

aviation The development, operation, and use of aircraft.

axis An imaginary line through the center of a body, such as Earth, that the body rotates about.

barometer An instrument used to measure air pressure.

barometric pressure See **air pressure**.

bellows A device used for producing a strong gust of air.

Bernoulli principle A natural law that states that, as the speed of a fluid moving over a surface increases, the pressure of the fluid on the surface decreases.

binoculars Two simple telescopes that are connected.

biology The study of organisms.

blast furnace A furnace that uses a steady blast of air to produce a fire hot enough to melt iron.

blood A liquid in the circulatory system that carries nutrients for growth and repair to cells and carries wastes away from cells.

blood vessels Tubes of the circulatory system through which blood flows.

bond Link together.

botanical gardens Areas in which plants are grown primarily for scientific studies and/or for viewing by the public.

botany The branch of biology that deals with the study of plants.

bronze An alloy of copper and tin that is easily shaped.

Bronze Age A period of prehistory between the Stone Age and the Iron Age when people used tools made of bronze.

buoyancy The tendency of an object to float in a liquid or rise in a gas.

buoyant force An upward force exerted by a fluid on an object partially or totally submerged in the fluid.

burning See combustion.

cadaver A dead body.

calendar A system for reckoning time by dividing it into days, weeks, months, and years.

calx The name used for the crumbly residue that remains after an object burns; ash.

canning A process of preserving food by heating it in airtight containers.

capillaries Small blood vessels that connect arteries and veins.

cast To pour melted materials into molds for desired shapes.

celestial bodies Natural things in the sky, such as stars, suns, moons, and planets.

cells Building blocks of organisms.

charcoal A carbon material used to make steel and to build fires.

chemical potential energy Energy tied up on chemical molecules.

chemical reaction The changing of a substance to a new substance.

chemistry The study of matter, including what substances are made of and how they change and combine.

chromatography A method of separating a mixture into its different substance.

circulatory system A closed network through which blood and its contents travel.

circumference The distance around a circle.

circumnavigate To travel completely around, such as around Earth.

cold forging Hammering cold metal into shape.

combination chemical reaction A chemical reaction in which two or more substances combine to form one product.

combustion The rapid combination of a substance with oxygen accompanied by an immediate release of a significant amount of energy; commonly called **burning**.

compass An instrument that indicates direction on Earth's surface.

compound A substance made up of two or more different types of atoms.

compound microscope A microscope with two or more lenses.

compress To press together.

conclusion A statement relating the results of an experiment to the hypothesis.

contract To draw together.

cosmology The branch of astronomy that deals with the study of the universe as a whole, including its distant past and its future.

crescent The Moon phase when the lighted area resembles a ring segment with pointed ends.

cultivated To raise as a crop.

cylinder An object shaped like a can.

data Observations and/or measured facts.

day The time it takes the Earth to make one rotation on its axis.

decompose To separate into the basic parts that make up a substance.

deformation A change in the shape of an object.

density The mass per unit volume of a substance.

detergent Any substance that cleans, such as soap.

diffuse To spread freely.

displace To push out of place.

dissect To cut apart.

dissolve To break up and thoroughly mix with another substance, as salt in water.

ductile Able to be drawn into a wire.

dye A colored substance used to color materials, such as fabrics.

Earth science The study of the Earth.

elastic Able to return to the original shape after being stretched.

elastic limit   The most a material can be stretched and still return to its original size and shape without permanent deformation.

electric current   A flow of charges.

electromagnet   A magnet produced by an electric current.

element   (1) One of the fundamental substances of the universe—earth, air, fire, water and ether—identified by Aristotle; (2) A substance made up of one kind of atom.

ellipse   Oval shape.

elliptical   Oval.

energy   The ability to cause motion.

energy conversion   A change of energy from one form to another.

enzyme   A chemical found in organisms that can change the speed of a chemical.

equator   An imaginary line around Earth that is an equal distance between the poles and that divides Earth in half.

ether   A supposedly perfect substance of which heavenly bodies were believed by Aristotle to be composed.

evaporate   To change from a liquid to a gas.

expand   To become greater in size.

experiment   A procedure to test a hypothesis.

extract   To remove, as metal from ore.

eyepiece   The lens the user looks through on an instrument such as a telescope.

fade   To get lighter in color.

finite   Having limits.

first quarter   The Moon phase following new moon, when in the Northern Hemisphere the right half of the side of the Moon facing Earth is lighted.

flight   The ability to move with direction through the air.

fluid   A gas or liquid.

focal point   A point within a telescope where light rays come together.

focus (plural **foci**)   Either of two points in line with each other on either side of the center point of an ellipse.

forging   A method of shaping heated metals by hammering.

free fall   The fall of an object in which gravity is the only force pulling it down.

freeze-drying   A method of preserving food by freezing it in a vacuum.

friction   A force that opposes the motion of an object whose surface is in contact with another object.

front   A boundary between air masses of different temperature or density.

fuel   A substance that will burn to produce energy.

fulcrum   The support about which a level turns.

full moon   The phase of the Moon when the side of the Moon facing Earth is fully lighted.

galaxy   A group made up of millions of stars, gas, and dust.

geocentric   Earth-centered.

gibbous moon   The Moon phase when more than half of the side of the Moon facing Earth is lighted.

glide   To move smoothly and effortlessly.

gondola   A basketlike passenger compartment suspended below an airship.

gravitational potential energy   Stored mechanical energy or potential energy due to the height of an object above a surface.

gravity   The force of attraction between all object in the universe.

gravity rate (G.R.)   The surface gravity of a celestial body divided by Earth's (Earth's G.R. equals 1).

Gregorian calendar   The modern calendar introduced in 1582 by Pope Gregory XIII.

hang glider   A kitelike flying craft.

hard water   Water that is rich in the minerals calcium, magnesium, and/or iron.

heart   The part of the circulatory system that pumps blood.

heliocentric   Sun-centered.

hemoglobin   A chemical in blood that gives it its red color and that is responsible for the ability of red blood cells to transport oxygen from the lungs to every part of the body.

herbarium (plural **herbaria**)   A collection of pressed, dried plants used for scientific study.

heretic   Someone who publicly disagrees with beliefs of the church.

histology The microscopic study of animal and plant parts.

horizon A circular line that forms the boundary where the sky and Earth appear to meet.

hour The period of time equal to one twenty-fourth of a solar day.

humidity The amount of water in the air.

hypertension High blood pressure.

hypothesis An idea about the solution to a problem.

ignition stimulus A source of energy that will raise a fuel to the temperature at which it will catch fire.

image A likeness of an object, such as that formed by a lens or mirror.

immiscible Unmixable.

indigo A blue dye made from indigofera and woad.

Industrial Age A time of incredible development in technology, from the late 1700 to the present day.

infinite Without limits.

insoluble Not able to be dissolved.

insulate To restrict the flow of heat.

Iron Age The period after the Bronze Age, when tools were mainly made of iron.

jet streams High-speed winds moving from west to east in the upper part of the troposphere at altitudes of about 6 miles (9.6 km).

Julian calendar A calendar established by Roman statesman Julius Caesar in 46 B.C. that was the first calendar based on the solar year and that established the number of days in the year and the order of the days of the week as they exist in present-day calendar.

Keplerian telescope See **refracting telescope.**

kinetic energy Energy that a moving object has because of its motion.

latex A milky liquid in specialized cells of plants.

law of conservation of matter A natural law that states that substances are not created or destroyed, only changed from one form to another.

leap year A year with 366 days which occurs every fourth year.

lever A simple machine that is used to move a load and that consists of a rigid bar, such as a tree limb, that turns about a fulcrum.

lever arm The distance a weight is from the fulcrum of a lever.

lift An upward force on a flying object.

lodestone See **magnetite.**

longitude Location along an imaginary line from Earth's North Pole to its South Pole.

lunar month The period of time from one new moon to the next; about 29½ days.

machine A tool used to make it easier to move things.

magnet An object with a strong magnetic field around it.

magnetic field The space around a magnet that attracts magnetic materials such as iron.

magnetic force The attraction between magnets or between a magnet and a magnetic material; also called **magnetism.**

magnetic lines of force A pattern of lines representing the magnetic field around a magnet.

magnetic materials Materials contain iron, cobalt, and/or nickel that can be attracted to or turned into a magnet.

magnetic north pole A place near Earth's North Pole where the north pole of an compass needle or any free-swinging magnet points.

magnetic south pole A place near Earth's South Pole where the south pole of a compass needle or any free-swinging magnet points.

magnetism See magnetic force.

magnetite An iron ore and a natural magnet; called **lodestone** in the past.

malleable Capable of being shaped by hammering.

mass An amount of material.

matter Anything that can be moved, takes up space, and has mass.

mauve A bluish purple dye.

mechanical energy The energy of moving objects— mechanical kinetic energy or of objects capable of motion—mechanical potential energy.

medicinal Concerning the healing properties of a plant or animal.

mer See **monomer.**

mercury barometer A type of barometer that uses changes in the height of mercury to indicate air pressure.

metallurgy The science of metals, including understanding the properties of different metals, removing metals from rocks, and working with metals.

meteorite   A rock from space that hits Earth's surface.

meteorologist   A scientist who studies weather.

meteorology   The study of weather.

microbes   Organisms visible only with a microscope and often associated with disease.

microgravity environment   An environment in which an object's apparent weight is small compared to its actual weight due to gravity.

microscope   An instrument used to magnify tiny or microscopic objects.

microscopic   Not visible to the naked eye.

molecule   A substance that can be further divided into atoms and is made up of two or more atoms bonded together.

monomer   Any of many small, repeating units in a polymer; also called a **mer**.

mordant   A chemical that fabric is soaked in to make the dye less likely to be washed out or fade.

native metals   Metals, such as gold and copper, that naturally occur in pure from, meaning they are not combined with other substances.

natural rubber   An elastic, water-repellent substance that comes form the latex of some plants.

natural satellites   Celestial bodies that orbit planets and stars (suns).

nerve   Fiber that sends messages form the body to and from the brain.

new moon   The phase of the Moon when the side of the Moon facing Earth is not lighted.

newton (N)   The SI unit of weight force, named after Sir Isaac Newton.

Newtonian telescope   See **reflecting telescope**.

Northern Hemisphere   The region of Earth north of the equator.

North Pole   The northernmost point on Earth.

north pole   The end of a compass needle or any free-swinging magnet that points toward the magnetic north pole of Earth.

nuclear reaction   A production of a new element through changes in an atom's nucleus.

nucleus   The center part of an atom.

objective lens   The lens of a refracting telescope that faces the object being viewed and gathers the light.

oblate spheroid   A sphere that is flattened at the poles and bulging at the equator.

orbit   (1) To move in a curved path about another body; (2) The curved path of one body revolving around another.

ore   A rock that contains enough metal to make it profitable to extract the metal.

organisms   Living things, such as plants and animals.

ornithopter   A wing-flapping aircraft.

oxidation   The process by which oxygen combines with a substance.

oxidizer   A source of oxygen.

pendulum   A suspended object that is free to swing back and forth.

percussion   A technique of tapping on the body, generally the chest, back, or abdomen, to diagnose illness.

perihelion   The closest point to the Sun in a planet's orbit.

petroglyphs   Carvings or line drawings on rock.

pharmacology   The study of medicines.

phases   The regularly recurring changes in the shape of the lighted part of a celestial body, such as a planet or the moon, facing Earth.

philosophers   People who study the meaning of life, problems of right and wrong, and how we know things.

phlogiston   A material substance that was believed to escape when something was burned.

photosynthesis   The process by which plants in the presence of light make food.

physics   The study of energy and matter and how they interact.

physiology   The study of life processes.

pickling   A method of preserving food in vinegar.

pigment   Coloring matter.

planets   Celestial bodies that orbit a sun.

plasma   The liquid part of blood.

poles   Ends of objects; see north pole and south pole and North Pole and South Pole.

polymer   Any substance consisting of large molecules that are made up of many monomers.

potash   A chemical found in the ash of wood that in the past was used in soap making.

potential energy   Energy of position or condition of an object that can be changed into kinetic energy.

pound   The English unit of weight.

prehistory   The time before written records appeared, which occurred about 3000 B.C.

preservatives   Food additives used to maintain freshness and extend the shelf life of package foods.

prism   A solid see-through material that changes the direction of light passing through.

problem   A scientific question to be solved.

propulsion   A means of moving an object.

proton   A positively charged particle in an atom's nucleus.

pulse   A regular beating in the arteries caused by the pulsing of blood after each contraction of the heart.

qualitative   Expressed as a quality or characteristic.

quantitative   Expressed as a quantity.

radioactive   Giving off a type of energy that is very dangerous to humans.

radiosonde   An instrument, carried by a balloon into the atmosphere, that measures temperature, pressure, and humidity and sends the information back to Earth by radio.

reckoning   To count or to calculate.

red blood cells   Cells in the blood that transport oxygen from the lungs to every part of the body.

reflecting telescope   A telescope that uses a combination of mirrors and lenses; also called a **Newtonian telescope.**

refracting telescope   A telescope that uses only lenses; also called a **Keplerian telescope.**

refrigerant   A cooling substance used in refrigeration.

refrigeration   A process of preserving by cooling.

repel   To cause to be pushed way from.

research   The process of collecting information about a topic being studied.

revolve   To orbit a body or center point.

rotate   To turn around a center point.

rubber   A term coined by Joseph Priestly, and used today for materials that have the unique property of high elasticity.

rust   Iron oxide, a reddish brown power.

rusting   The slow oxidation of any substance, with small amounts of energy given.

satellite   A body that orbits a planet or star (sun). See **artificial satellite** or **natural satellite.**

science   A system of knowledge about the nature of the things in the universe.

scientific method   The process of thinking through possible solutions to a problem and testing each possibility to find the best solution.

seasonal year   See **solar year.**

skeleton   A structural framework made of bone that supports the body and allows it to move.

smelting   Melting ores to separate the metals.

soap scum   A gray, waxy solid that is insoluble in water, forms what is commonly called a "bathtub ring."

soft water   Water that is poor in the minerals calcium, magnesium, and/or iron.

solar day   The period of time from midnight to midnight; 24 hours.

solar system   A group of celestial bodies that orbit a star called a sun.

solar year   The time it takes the Earth to revolve about the Sun; 365 days, 5 hours and 48 minutes, and 45 seconds; also called a **seasonal year.**

South Pole   The most southern region of Earth.

south pole   The end of a compass needle or any free-swinging magnet that points toward the magnetic south pole of Earth.

spherical   Ball-shaped.

spheroid   A sphere that is flattened at the poles and bulging at the equator.

spinal cord   A bundle of nerves running through the center of the spine.

spine   Backbone.

square   An object having four equal sides.

stars   Large celestial bodies made of very hot, glowing gases. The Sun is the closet star to Earth.

steel   An iron alloy made of iron and carbon.

stethoscope   An instrument that helps physicians to better hear body sounds.

stoma (plural **stomata**)   A hole in a leaf, through which gases, such as water vapor, pass.

Stone Age   A period of time from about 2 million years ago to about 5000 B.C.

storm   A fast-moving air mass.

substance   A material made of one kind of matter.

supersonic   Faster than the speed of sound.

surface gravity   Gravity at or near the surface of a celestial body.

swim bladder   A special balloonlike body part in fish that helps them rise or sink by increasing or decreasing the volume of air in the swim bladder.

synthetic   Man-made.

synthetic rubber   Man-made rubber made from materials such as petroleum.

technology   The use of scientific knowledge to make useful items.

telescope   An instrument that makes a distant object appear nearer and larger by using lenses and often mirrors to gather light and form an image of the object.

temperature   How hot or cold something is.

thermometer   An instrument used to measurer temperature.

third quarter   The Moon phase following full moon, when in the Northern Hemisphere the left half of the side of the Moon facing Earth is lighted.

toxic   Poisonous.

transpiration   The process by which plants lose water through their leaves.

troposphere   The layer of the atmosphere nearest the surface of the Earth.

turbine   A wheel that changes the force of a moving fluid into mechanical energy.

universe   Earth and all natural objects in space regarded as a whole.

vacuum   A space form which gases have been removed.

vapor   A gas formed from a substance that is usually a solid or a liquid at room temperature.

vaporize   To change to a gas.

veins   Blood vessels that carry oxygen-poor blood from the body to the heart.

venules   Small blood vessels that connect capillaries with veins.

verdigris   A thin green coating on copper or copper alloys such as bronze.

vernal equinox   The first day of spring, on or about March 21.

vertebra   (plural vertebrae) One of the small bones that make up the spine.

volume   The amount of space that a material occupies.

vulcanization   The process of heating a mixture of rubber and sulfur.

wane   To decrease in quantity, as a waning Moon decreases in the amount of the visible lighted area.

wax   To increase in quantity, as a waxing Moon increases in the amount of the visible lighted area.

weather   The condition of Earth's atmosphere in a specific place at a particular time.

week   A seven-day period of time.

weight   The measure of gravitational force on an object.

work   The transfer of energy that occurs when a force causes an object to move.

wrought iron   A mixture of iron and sand contains glasslike threads throughout, making the iron malleable and easily forged.

year   See **solar year.**

zoology   The study of animals.

Index

GREYSCALE

BIN TRAVELER FORM

Cut By _Dina Lopez_   Qty 32   Date 08-14-24

Scanned By _(signature)_   Qty   Date Cut 8-24

Scanned Batch IDs

5628017442.

Notes / Exception